EVENTS THAT CHANG[ED]

The Story of the

WWI Armistice

100 Years Later

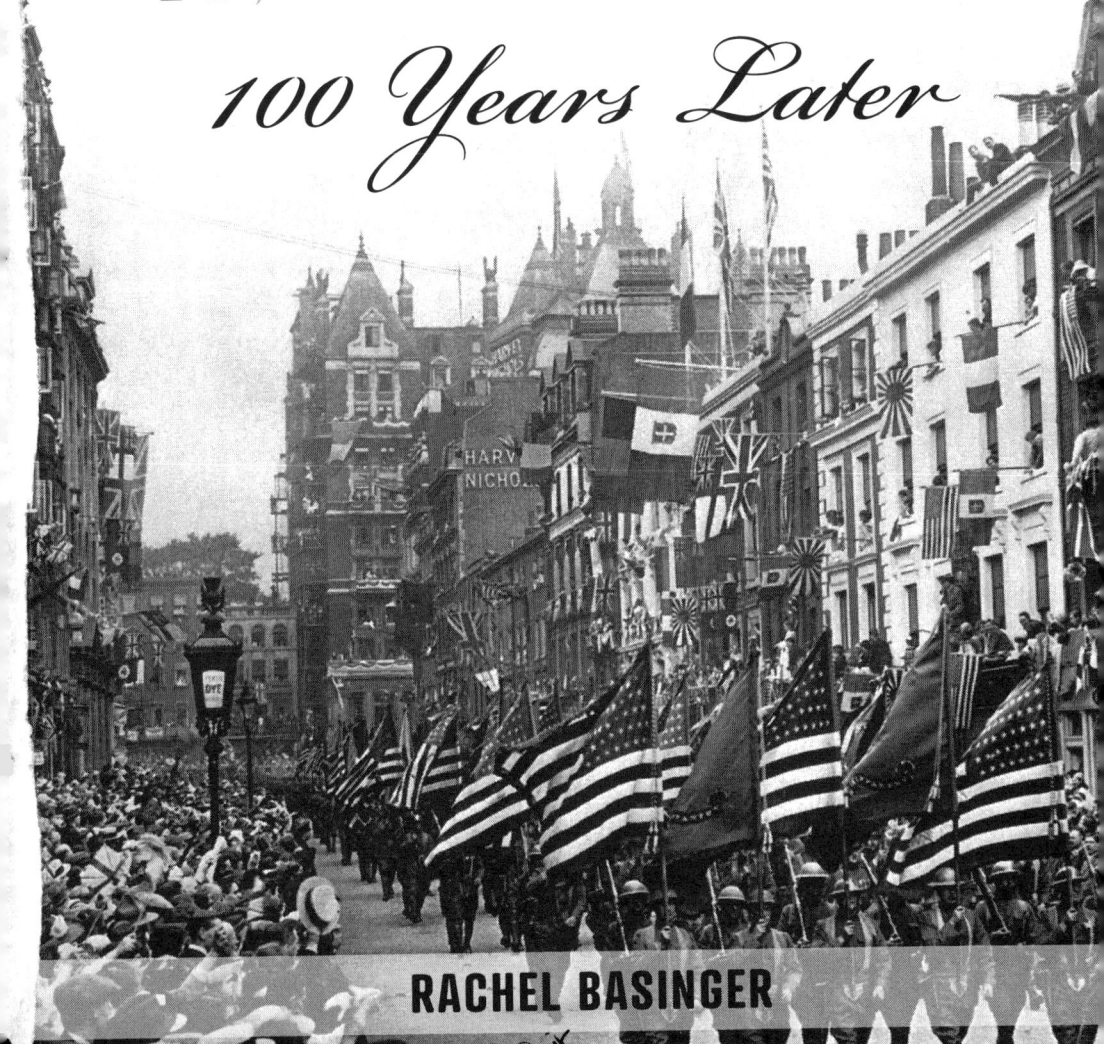

RACHEL BASINGER

EVENTS THAT CHANGED THE COURSE OF HISTORY: THE STORY OF THE WWI ARMISTICE 100 YEARS LATER

Copyright © 2017 Atlantic Publishing Group, Inc.

1405 SW 6th Avenue • Ocala, Florida 34471 • Phone 800-814-1132 • Fax 352-622-1875
Website: www.atlantic-pub.com • Email: sales@atlantic-pub.com
SAN Number: 268-1250

No part of this publication may be reproduced, stored in a retrieval system, or transmitted in any form or by any means, electronic, mechanical, photocopying, recording, scanning, or otherwise, except as permitted under Section 107 or 108 of the 1976 United States Copyright Act, without the prior written permission of the Publisher. Requests to the Publisher for permission should be sent to Atlantic Publishing Group, Inc., 1405 SW 6th Avenue, Ocala, Florida 34471.

Library of Congress Cataloging-in-Publication Data

Names: Basinger, Rachel, 1992- author.
Title: Events that changed the course of history : the story of the WWI armistice 100 years later / by Rachel Basinger.
Other titles: Story of the WWI armistice 100 years later
Description: Ocala, Florida : Atlantic Publishing Group, Inc., 2017. | Includes bibliographical references and index.
Identifiers: LCCN 2017041526| ISBN 9781620234204 (pbk. : alk. paper) | ISBN 9781620234198 (hardcover : alk. paper) | ISBN 1620234203 (alk. paper)
Subjects: LCSH: World War, 1914-1918—Armistices.
Classification: LCC D641 .B37 2017 | DDC 940.3/12—dc23 LC record available at https://lccn.loc.gov/2017041526

LIMIT OF LIABILITY/DISCLAIMER OF WARRANTY: The publisher and the author make no representations or warranties with respect to the accuracy or completeness of the contents of this work and specifically disclaim all warranties, including without limitation warranties of fitness for a particular purpose. No warranty may be created or extended by sales or promotional materials. The advice and strategies contained herein may not be suitable for every situation. This work is sold with the understanding that the publisher is not engaged in rendering legal, accounting, or other professional services. If professional assistance is required, the services of a competent professional should be sought. Neither the publisher nor the author shall be liable for damages arising herefrom. The fact that an organization or Web site is referred to in this work as a citation and/or a potential source of further information does not mean that the author or the publisher endorses the information the organization or Web site may provide or recommendations it may make. Further, readers should be aware that Internet Web sites listed in this work may have changed or disappeared between when this work was written and when it is read.

TRADEMARK DISCLAIMER: All trademarks, trade names, or logos mentioned or used are the property of their respective owners and are used only to directly describe the products being provided. Every effort has been made to properly capitalize, punctuate, identify, and attribute trademarks and trade names to their respective owners, including the use of ® and ™ wherever possible and practical. Atlantic Publishing Group, Inc. is not a partner, affiliate, or licensee with the holders of said trademarks.

Printed in the United States

PROJECT MANAGER: Danielle Lieneman
INTERIOR LAYOUT AND JACKET DESIGN: Nicole Sturk

Reduce. Reuse. RECYCLE.

A decade ago, Atlantic Publishing signed the Green Press Initiative. These guidelines promote environmentally friendly practices, such as using recycled stock and vegetable-based inks, avoiding waste, choosing energy-efficient resources, and promoting a no-pulping policy. We now use 100-percent recycled stock on all our books. The results: in one year, switching to post-consumer recycled stock saved 24 mature trees, 5,000 gallons of water, the equivalent of the total energy used for one home in a year, and the equivalent of the greenhouse gases from one car driven for a year.

Over the years, we have adopted a number of dogs from rescues and shelters. First there was Bear and after he passed, Ginger and Scout. Now, we have Kira, another rescue. They have brought immense joy and love not just into our lives, but into the lives of all who met them.

We want you to know a portion of the profits of this book will be donated in Bear, Ginger and Scout's memory to local animal shelters, parks, conservation organizations, and other individuals and nonprofit organizations in need of assistance.

*– **Douglas & Sherri Brown,***
President & Vice-President of Atlantic Publishing

Table of Contents

Prelude 9

Chapter 1: Facts Everyone Should Know About the Great War 13

Chapter 2: The Course of the Great War 19

Chapter 3: The Weeks Leading Up to the Armistice 51

Chapter 4: Signing the Armistice 69

Chapter 5: The Hours Before the Armistice Took Effect 73

Chapter 6: Individual Responses to the Armistice 85

Chapter 7: Celebrations Around the World 93

Chapter 8: Paris Peace Conference 105

Chapter 9: Military Leaders and Politicians After World War I 119

Chapter 10: Conclusion (The Aftermath of the Armistice) 133

Author's Note/Acknowledgements 151

Historical Timeline 155

Glossary 157

Bibliography 163

About the Author 171

Index 173

Dedication:
To Dr. David Stewart for teaching me to love history (and Spain)

11 a.m. on November 11. For those who knew (and not all soldiers did because their commanders did not want the field to erupt into celebrations), their wristwatches came in handy. Never had two numbers — two toothpicks or two stick legs on a stick figure — meant so much. Those two thin numbers would usher in a time of stillness, peace, celebration, mourning, and homecoming. For the millions of soldiers who had fought without respite for the past four years of 1914 to 1918, they almost could not imagine the atmosphere the armistice and 11 a.m. would bring. They had grown too used to constant fighting, exploding shells, dripping rain, dying buddies, and infested trenches.

Back in Kent in the United Kingdom, a young woman named Ethel Mary Bilbrough woke up on Monday, November 11, feeling an auspicious aura in the air. Several seconds later, BANG! Ethel assumed that it was yet another raid when another explosion shook the windows and "the guns started frantically firing all round us like an almighty fugue."[1] At that point, Ethel knew that the putative (so-called) raid was wrong and that instead the armistice had been signed: "The end had come at last, and the greatest war in history was over."[2]

Much of the Western world, detached from the battlefields, celebrated, and pandemonium dominated the streets. Bells chimed, guns thundered, and people cheered, shouted, and sang. The Great War was finally over.

For those on the battlefield, however, they had endured six hours of fighting from 5 a.m. when the armistice was signed to 11 a.m. when the armistice took effect. Over 2,500 men died in those last six hours, some of whom had survived all four years of the war, only to die minutes before the armistice took effect.

Thus, the World War I Armistice brought both celebration and mourning: relief that the war had ended but sadness that it had taken so many lives, even on the last day of the war.

1. Alston.
2. Alston.

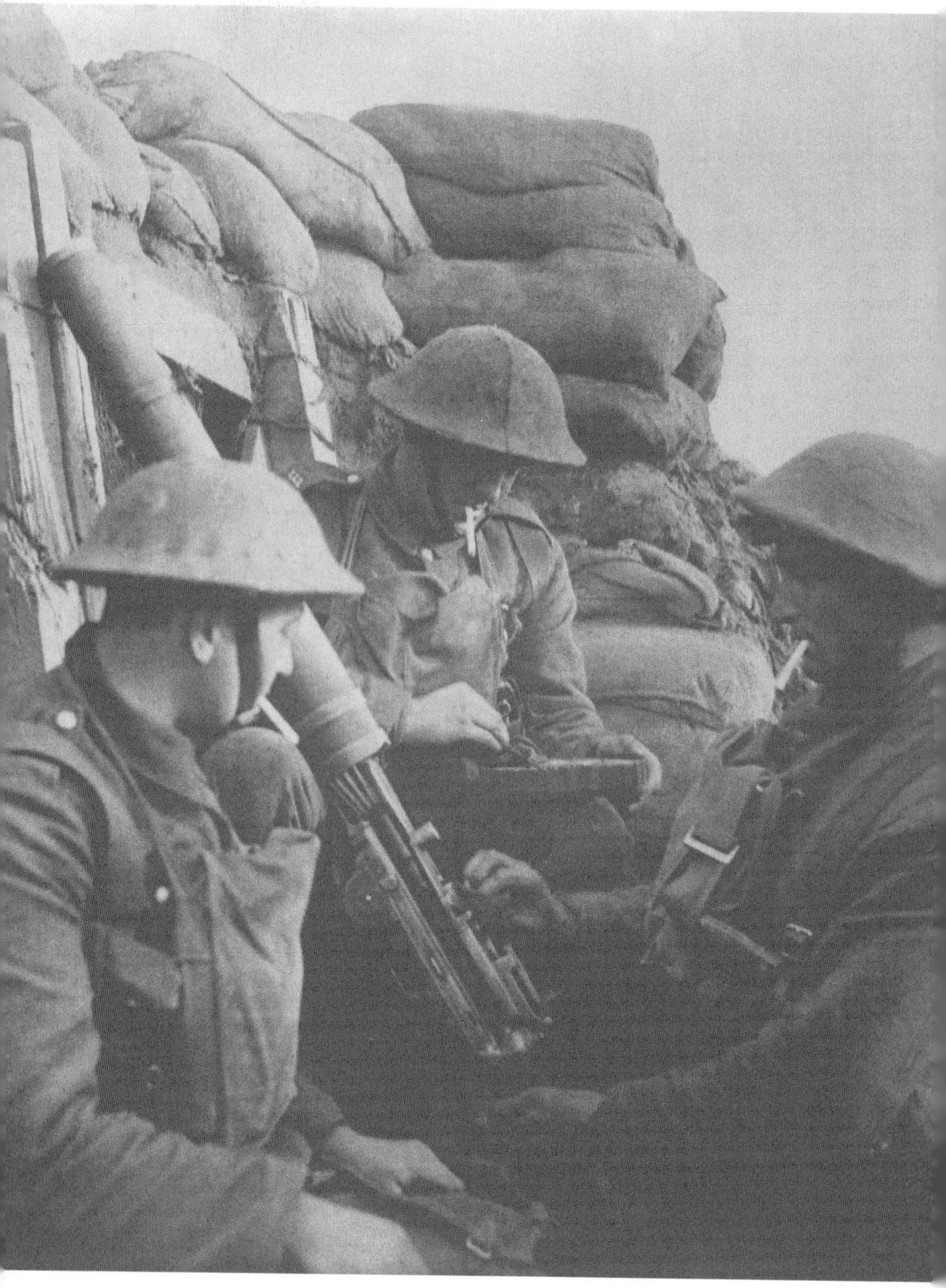

CHAPTER 1

Facts Everyone Should Know About the Great War

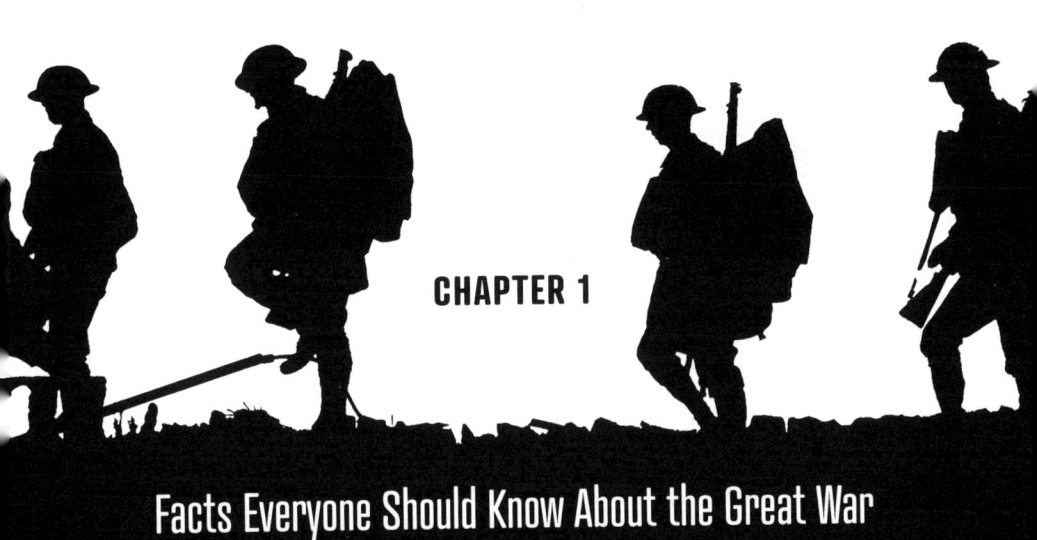

"The war that will end war"

Imagine you are a college freshman on the first day of classes, sitting in the first row in the classroom for your Western Civilization class. Your professor asks you and the rest of the class what you know about World War I. While the rest of the class racks their brains trying to remember details about it, you don't need to because you already know a lot about the war, including that it was originally called the Great War! While the other chapters of this book will follow a chronological focus of World War I, emphasizing specifically the end of the war and the Armistice that took effect on the eleventh hour of the eleventh day of the eleventh month in 1918 (11 a.m. on November 11, 1918), this chapter offers a broad overview of the war with important facts that everyone should know about the Great War.

While history is certainly more than just dates, you need to know some dates, especially those that have a special significance to the United States and to the world. Every American should know that the Great War began in 1914, that it ended in 1918, and that the Americans did not join the war until 1917. In fact, the British and French soldiers referred to Americans as "Johnny-come-latelies" and dud shells as "Wilsons" because President Woodrow Wilson took a while to enter the war.

World War I is often referred to as "the war to end all wars" because its participants had such high hopes for bringing permanent peace after the war. The phrase actually comes from H.G. Wells, who penned an article for *The Daily News* in August 1914 after the outbreak of the Great War, entitled "The War That Will End War." In October 1914, Wells published it as a book and argued that it would be the last war humanity would fight: "For this is now a war for peace. It aims straight at disarmament. It aims at a settlement that shall stop this sort of thing for ever. Every soldier who fights against Germany now is a crusader against war. This, the greatest of all wars, is not just another war — it is the last war!"[3]

---

3. Wells, 1914.

> **Did you know?**
>
> According to the Oxford English Dictionary, the phrase "Johnny-come-lately" originated in the United States in the 1800s and referred to a newcomer and sometimes to a new recruit or a novice.

At the beginning of the war in 1914, the Allied Powers consisted of Serbia, Russia, France, and Great Britain. Later, Montenegro; Belgium; Japan; Italy, which should have officially joined the Central Powers due to the Triple Alliance of 1882; Portugal; Romania; the United States; Greece; Siam, which is now known as Thailand; and others joined. By contrast, the Central Powers included fewer nations. It originally comprised of Germany and Austria-Hungary. The Ottoman Empire and Bulgaria joined later. While the Great War involved over twenty countries from five different continents, excluding Antarctica and South America, actual fighting took place on three continents: Europe, Africa, and Asia.

> **Fun Fact**
>
> Entente is a French word that means an understanding, often between a group of states or powers. It was used frequently in the 1800s and 1900s. The Triple Entente refers to an understanding between the Russian Empire, France, and the United Kingdom of Great Britain and Ireland that linked these three countries in 1907.

Many consider the Great War to be the first "modern" war because the war featured radio usage, war planes, tanks, submarines, and poison gas. Due in part to this new technology, World War I was one of the bloodiest wars in history, and many consider the war as extremely unnecessary. Known for trench warfare, the Great War included several prominent battles that we will discuss in detail later, such as Ypres, Gallipoli, Jutland, Verdun, Somme, and Amiens. The Treaty of Versailles, signed at the Paris Peace Conference in 1919, was extremely punitive toward the Germans — as was the November 11, 1918 Armistice — and many believe that the stringent measures in the treaty played a large role in the rise of Nazism and World War II.

Although World War II certainly overshadowed the Great War in terms of total mobilized forces and casualties — including killed in action (KIA), wounded in action (WIA), and missing in action (MIA), the World War I casualty figures are still staggering. Over 65 million men served on both sides, and of those men, 37.5 million were casualties, including 8.5 million deaths. In total, 57.5 percent of all active forces were casualties with some countries, such as Austria-Hungary, suffering a 90 percent casualty rate and others, such as the United States, suffering only a 7 percent casualty rate.[4] It is also estimated that over 6 million civilians were killed during the war.

---

4. "The Great War — Casualties and Deaths."

Comparatively, the mortality rate was almost always higher for the World War I in contrast to World War II although the losses from 1914-1918 were on par with total war losses in Europe from 1792-1815.[5] Only the USSR/Russia had higher losses during World War II, in large part due to Josef Stalin.[6]

The Western Front was the primary focus of the war, and that front experienced 11 million casualties, over 3 million deaths and over 7.5 million injuries. The majority of the battles in World War I took place on the Western Front in an area about 85 miles wide, meaning that over 3 million men died on a plot of land the width of Maryland.

It should be noted that this book will use the terms "First World War," "World War I," and "The Great War" interchangeably. You should remember that in 1914 there had been no Second World War, so many people referred to the conflict of 1914 to 1918 as The Great War or the World War. It is anachronistic to refer to World War I as such, but such a name does help us remember the deep consequences the war had for the twentieth century and the way it led to World War II.

Prominent Politicians	Prominent Generals
Austria-Hungary: Emperor Franz Josef	Austria-Hungary: Field Marshal Conrad von Hötzendorf and General Svetozar Boroević
France: President Raymond Poincaré	France: Marshal Joseph Joffre, General Robert Nivelle, General Philippe Pétain, and Marshal Ferdinand Foch

---

5. Audoin-Rouzeau and Becker, 2002.
6. Audoin-Rouzeau and Becker, 2002.

Prominent Politicians	Prominent Generals
Germany: Kaiser Wilhelm II	Germany: General Helmuth von Moltke, General Erich von Falkenhayn, Field Marshal Paul von Hindenburg, and General Erich Ludendorff
Great Britain: Sir Edward Grey, Lord Kitchener, and Prime Minister David Lloyd George	Great Britain: Field Marshal Douglas Haig
Russia: Czar Nicholas II	Russia: General Aleksei Brusilov
United States: President Woodrow Wilson	United States: General John J. Pershing

CHAPTER 2

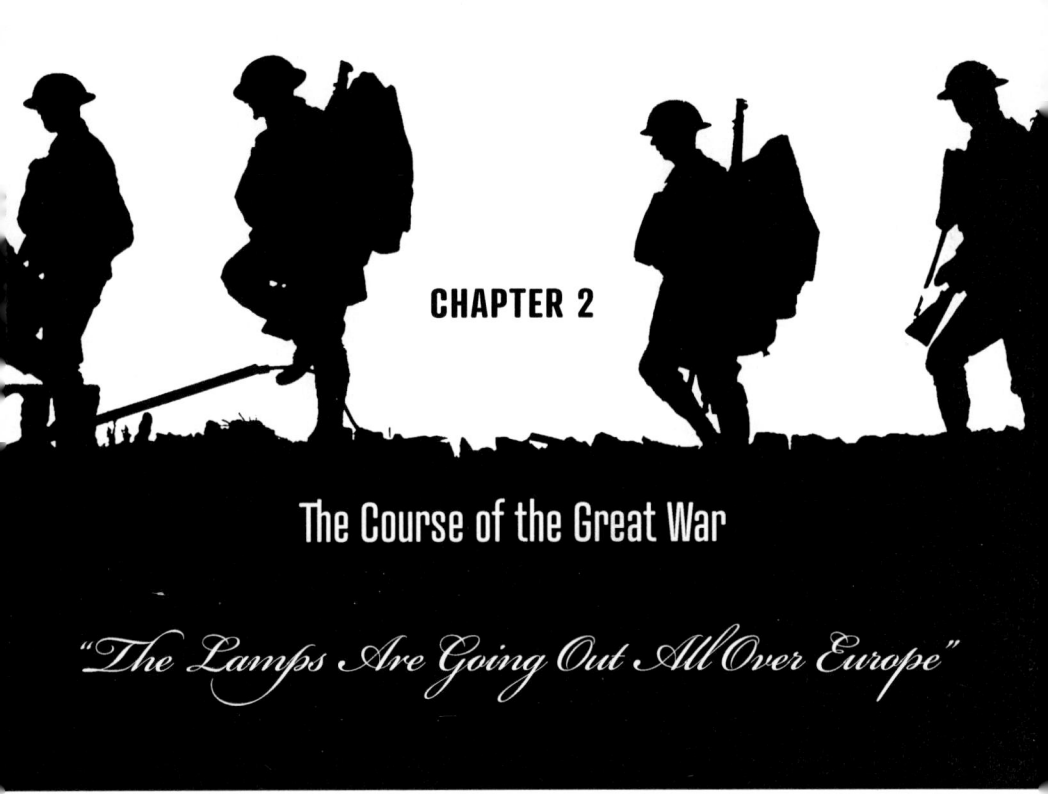

The Course of the Great War

"The Lamps Are Going Out All Over Europe"

Although the Great War was the first of two world wars, its cause was actually quite regional. Throughout European history, various nationalities have coexisted in the different countries and regions. Eastern Europe in particular was home to numerous ethnic groups with distinctive religions, languages, and culture. Austria-Hungary in particular had a conglomeration of diverse nationalities. In 1908, Austria-Hungary had annexed Bosnia-Herzegovina, which greatly angered the Serbs because they wanted to create a large Serbian kingdom that included the southern Slavs. In other words, the Serbs felt that they had a closer connection with Bosia-Herzegovina than Austria-Hungary. After the Balkan Wars of 1912-1913, Serbia had grown as a country, and Austria-Hungary feared Serbia's strength. Although the Bosnian Slavs identified more with the Serbs, Austria-Hungary wanted to keep the Slavs in its empire of 50 million people and did not want them to join Serbia, which had 3 million people. Hardline conservatives in Austria wanted to crush Serbia because they feared it was getting too powerful. The person holding everything together was Archduke Franz Ferdinand, the heir apparent to the Austro-Hungarian throne then occupied by Emperor Franz Josef, an octogenarian or person in his eighties.

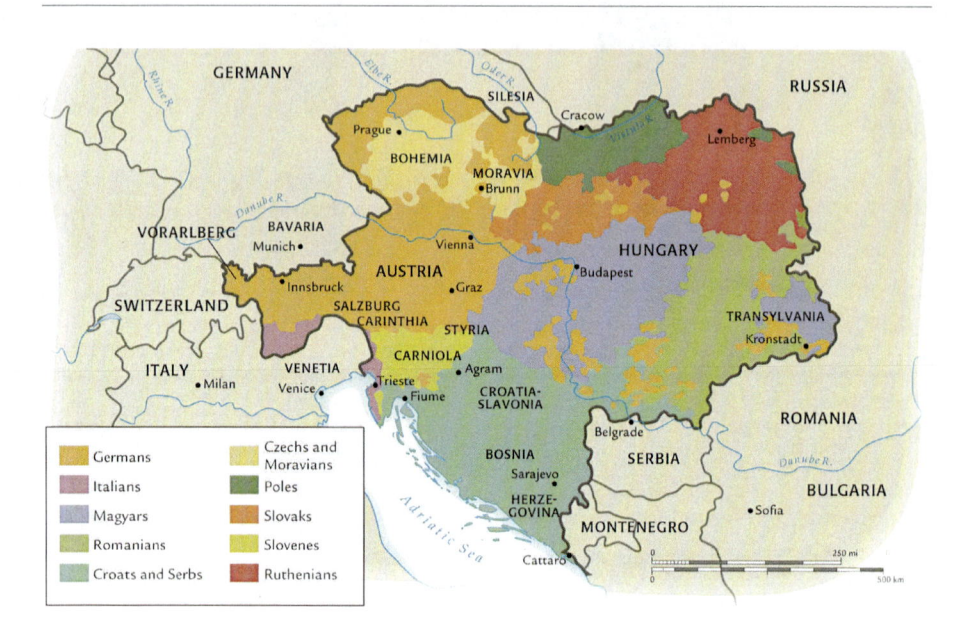

> **Fun Fact**
>
> Conservative meant something different in the 1800s and early 1900s. While today we think of a conservative as a Republican who strongly supports the military, tends to be nationalist, and wants to cut taxes and balance the budget, that was not the case in 1914. Conservatives then were traditional, supported the monarchy and the church, did not like nationalism, and did not like radical change. An extremely prominent conservative in the 1800s was Austrian Klemens von Metternich. Austria, along with Russia, was one of the most conservative European nations in the 1800s and early 1900s.

On June 28, 1914, Serbia's National Day, the Archduke and his wife, Countess Sophie Chotek, made an ill-fated visit to Sarajevo, the capital of Bosnia-Herzegovina, in an attempt to spread good will. Although the Serbian government had warned the Austrian government earlier about a plot to assassinate the Archduke by an ultranationalist Serbian group, Franz Ferdinand decided to proceed with his trip, even with a limited security force, because he did not see Sarajevo as a hostile city. Behind the plot was Ujedinjenjeili Smrt (Union or Death), an ultranationalist Serbian terrorist organization known popularly as the Black Hand. It was a radical version of Narodna Odbrana (National Defense), a terrorist organization founded in 1908 to oppose Austria's annexation of Bosnia-Herzegovina.[7] The Black Hand had trained and provided several young men with pistols and bombs to assassinate the Archduke; one of them was Gavrilo Princip, a nineteen-year-old born into a poor Bosnian Serb family who wanted to see a united Slavic nation.

Due to the topology of Sarajevo, anyone could easily deduce the route for Ferdinand's motorcade on June 28 by looking at the Miljacka River, which

---

7. McMeekin, 2014.

ran — or trickled during the summer — through the city. As historian Sean McMeekin notes, "Any royal procession would likely proceed down the Appelquai, the main avenue running parallel to the Miljacka."[8] On June 28, Gavrilo Princip was joined by five other assassins and the organizer, Ilitch. Princip, Grabezh, and Chabrinovitch came from Belgrade while Vaso Chubrilovitch, Cvjetko Popovitch, and Bosnian Muslim Mehmedbashitch were all locals.[9] Mehmedbashitch, Chubrilovitch, and Princip carried pistols, Chabrinovitch held a fuse bomb, but only Grabezh — at the end of the route — carried a bomb and a pistol in case the first four failed.

As the Archduke and his wife began their tour of the city in a six-car motorcade, one of the assassins threw a bomb, which hit the third car, and injured several people. The bomb thrower was seized after attempting to take poison, and all but Princip fled. One thought the plot was futile, and another felt sorry for Sophie. Princip stayed. The Archduke decided to continue with the tour, but with a revised route. Unfortunately, around 10:30 a.m., the driver took a wrong turn — although it would have been correct in the original route — and was told of his error. He attempted to correct his mistake, but he was unsuccessful. The Archduke's car paused right in front of Princip, who had been waiting there all morning. Twice Princip shot his pistol, an FN Model 1910 Browning semi-automatic, first hitting Sophie in the stomach and then piercing Franz Ferdinand in the neck.[10] Just before he died, the Archduke cried out to his wife, "Sophie!" The day of their deaths, June 28, 1914, was also their fourteenth anniversary. Princip was quickly arrested, tried for the two murders, and was found guilty. Nonetheless, he escaped execution because of his youth and was instead sentenced to imprisonment for twenty years. Interestingly, Princip died in April 1918, likely of tuberculosis.

---

8. McMeekin, 2014.
9. McMeekin, 2014.
10. McMeekin, 2014.

> **Did you know?**
>
> Many serious works of scholarship assert that Gavrilo Princip had just exited a deli and was eating a sandwich when he shot and killed the Archduke and his wife. In his 2013 University of Oxford podcast, "The Sandwich that Sabotaged Civilisation," Dr. Paul Miller, a Marie Curie Fellow at the University of Birmingham (U.K.) and associate professor of history at McDaniel College (U.S.), researched this story extensively and its connection to historical memory. He noted that well-known historian Mark Dash likely found the origin of this myth: a historical documentary, "Days That Shook the World," first shown in 2003. Dr. Miller also observed that sandwiches did not exist in Sarajevo in 1914 and that none of the eyewitnesses, including Princip himself, mention food, eating, or sandwiches in any of their accounts.

Emperor Franz Josef was outraged at the death of the Archduke and considered it ample reason to punish Serbia, which he called a "dangerous little viper." Franz Josef knew that Russia would most likely support Serbia and that Austria-Hungary could not take on Russia alone. After Sarajevo, the Austro-Hungarian Foreign Minister drew up a letter for the emperor to sign and send to Austria's ally Germany, asking for the Kaiser's assistance. On July 6, 1914, the Kaiser and Imperial Chancellor von Bethmann Hollweg sent a telegram in response, stating "that His Majesty will faithfully stand by Austria-Hungary, as is required by the obligations of his alliance and of his ancient friendship."[11] This telegram became the "blank check" through which Germany would assist Austria in defeating Serbia, no questions asked. In fact, although later deleted before sending the telegram, the original draft stated that the Kaiser would support Austria "under all circumstances."[12] Both Franz Josef and the Kaiser thought that Russia was not prepared to fight and expected the war to be short.

---

11. Montgelas and Schücking, 1924.
12. Montgelas and Schücking, 1924.

Of course, before Austria-Hungary could declare war on Serbia, it needed a *casus belli*, or an act justifying war. Thus, on July 23, 1914, Austria-Hungary sent an ultimatum of ten stringent demands to which Serbia had to agree within forty-eight hours. Surprisingly, Serbia agreed to all but one of the demands, the sixth requirement that stated the Austrian government would take part in the "judicial inquiry against every participant in the conspiracy of the twenty-eighth of June who may found in the Serbian territory."[13] Prominent government officials in several countries, including Sir Edward Grey of England and the German Minister for Foreign Affairs thought Serbia accepted much more than they anticipated. In fact, the Kaiser thought the Serbians had been extremely reasonable and that war had been avoided and stated, "A great moral victory for Vienna; but with it every reason for war disappears."[14]

---

13. Montgelas and Schücking, 1924.
14. Falls, 2014.

> **Fun Fact**
>
> In a telegram to another British politician on July 24, 1914, British foreign secretary Sir Edward Grey called the Austro-Hungarian ultimatum to Serbia "the most formidable document [he] had ever seen addressed by one State to another that was independent."[15]

Austria-Hungary, however, did not accept the Serbian response, as the Serbs had not agreed to *all* of the demands. On July 28, 1914, they declared war on Serbia. Russia began to mobilize on July 29 in defense of its ally, Serbia. In response, Germany mobilized on July 30 and demanded that Russia must demobilize in twelve hours or risk war. Not wanting to risk a two-front war, Germany inquired whether France intended to remain neutral, especially since Russia was connected to France in the Triple Entente. If France stayed neutral, Germany demanded the fortress cities of Verdun and Toul, designed specifically for French protection from Germany and also significant to France for cultural reasons.[16] Both Russia and France did not accept Germany's ultimatums. Thus, Germany declared war on Russia and France on August 1 and 3, respectively. In turn, Great Britain declared war on Germany on August 5 when the Germans refused to remove their troops from Belgium. Finally, on August 6, 1914, Austria-Hungary declared war on Russia. As Sir Edward Grey famously stated, "The lamps are going out all over Europe. We shall not see them lit again in our time."[17] Unlike Grey, most common people welcomed the war and held large, nationalistic parades to send their men off. Everyone expected the war to end before Christmas 1914.

---

15. Gooch and Temperley, 1926.
16. Persico, 2004.
17. Persico, 2004.

KARTE VON EUROPA IM JAHRE 1914

Gezeichnet von W. Trier

Different Reasons for Fighting	For Different Countries
Discipline Serbia	**Austria-Hungary**
Assist Austria-Hungary	**Germany**
Defend Belgian Neutrality	**Great Britain**
Assist Russia & Keep Verdun and Toul	**France**
Stand by Serbia	**Russia**

> **Did you know?**
>
> Many of the animosities held by European countries date back to the Franco-Prussian War of 1870-1871 when a coalition of German states led by Prussia handily crushed France. This defeat weakened France as a world power and led to the unification of Germany in 1871. Germany took some territory from France, including Alsace-Lorraine, which would serve as a sore point for years. The Great War was France's excuse to get back at Germany, and Germany intended to defend its honor and keep its conquests from the Franco-Prussian War.

Germany now faced the two-front war it had tried to avoid: one against France and the other against Russia. Fortunately, the Germans had a plan: the Schlieffen Plan, named after Field Marshal Alfred von Schlieffen, who crafted the plan in 1905. Germany would circumvent a two-front war by bypassing France's eastern defenses and going through Belgium. By going north of Brussels and then south to catch French forces going through Alsace-Lorraine, the counterclockwise wheeling motion of the plan would act as a giant pincer, four hundred miles wide. The Germans were so confident that the Schlieffen Plan would succeed that they planned to parade in Paris in 6 weeks on September 21, 1914.

The Germans, of course, had reason to be optimistic. They had amassed quite the army and navy in the 1910s. As home secretary, Winston Churchill, a lifelong Francophile, had attended both German and French army maneuvers and observed that the Germans easily bested the French. In true Churchill and British fashion, the then home secretary and later famous British Prime Minister during World War II retorted, "I can only thank God that there is a sea between England and Germany."[18]

---

18. Johnson, 2009.

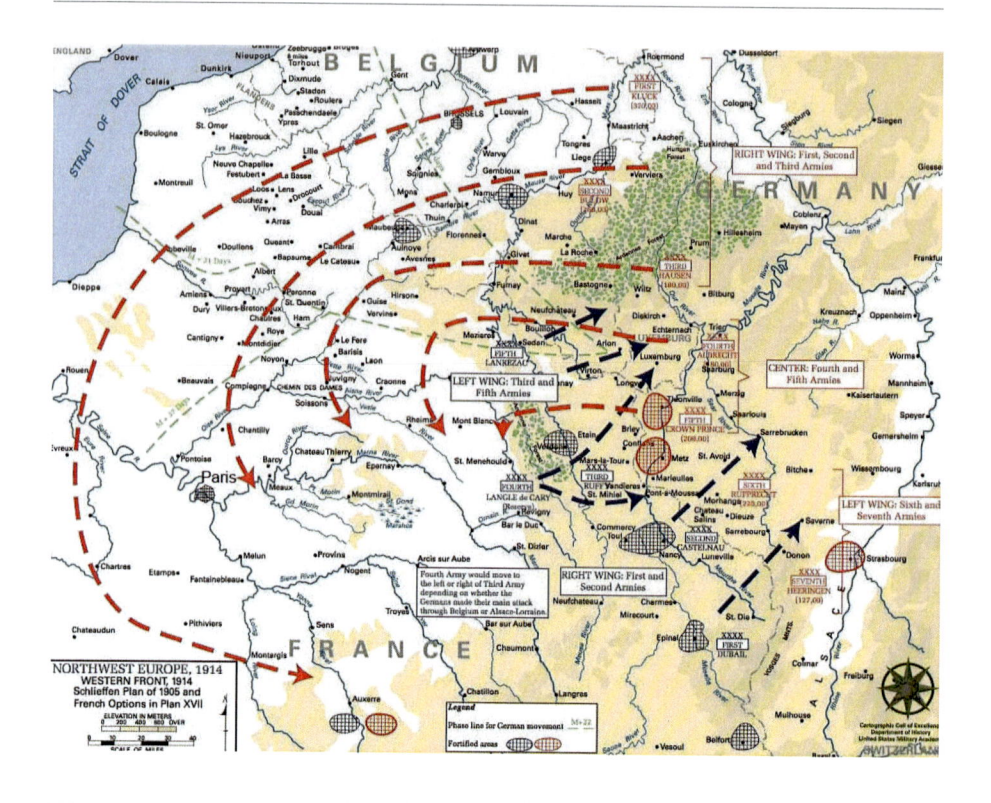

Did you know?

Great Britain, along with four other nations, had signed the Treaty of London in 1839 to guarantee Belgium's neutrality. After parliamentary debates in 1870, Britain maintained a moral obligation to defend Belgium, instead of a strict treaty requirement to give Britain the opportunity to decide what was in its best interest. On August 3, 1914, British foreign secretary Sir Edward Grey delivered a speech in the House of Commons, urging Britain to support both Belgium and France. Speaking of Belgium, Grey stated, "it is quite clear that there is an obligation on this country to do its utmost to prevent the consequences to which those facts will lead if they are undisputed."[19] Thus, Britain's concern for Belgium and unwillingness to let Germany dominate the European continent led Britain to enter the war on August 5, 1914.

---

19. Grey, 1914.

Fun Fact

The Germans did not have much regard for the Treaty of London, blatantly violating it despite British statements that it would declare war on Germany if the Germans violated Belgian neutrality. In fact, German Chancellor Theobald von Bethmann Hollweg referred to the Treaty of London of 1839 as a "scrap of paper."[20]

The plan, however, did not go as intended. Field Marshal Schlieffen had died in 1913, and his successor General von Moltke made some changes to the Schlieffen Plan. Scholars continue to debate whether the plan would have contributed to German success if it had stayed as written or if Moltke was correct in adjusting the plan, crafted in 1892, to new circumstances. In any case, the 90 percent of troops that Schlieffen had originally allotted in France was decreased to 60 percent. Of the remaining 40 percent, 15 percent was sent to defend East Prussia against Russia, and 25 percent went to defend Alsace-Lorraine against the French.[21] Beginning on September 5, 1914, the French checked the German advance during the First Battle of the Marne (September 5-12, 1914). The Germans were twenty miles from Paris, yet they could advance no farther.

---

20. Zuckerman, 2004.
21. Persico, 2004.

> ### Fun Fact
>
> The reason military offenses, like the Schlieffen Plan, were crafted in a counterclockwise motion dates back to the ancient Greeks! The phalanx, a rectangular mass military formation used by the Greeks (and later Romans), was composed of soldiers protected by their shield on the left side and a spear in their right hand. Moving counterclockwise allowed the phalanx to fight and stay protected as it moved. Paul Chrystal notes that Schlieffen was inspired by Hannibal and thought that Hannibal's maneuvers at Cannae would stay relevant in the twentieth century.[22] Thanks to Lieutenant Colonel Gil Petrina (ret.) for this insight!

Next began the unfortunately named "Race to the Sea." Oddly, it was not so much a race as French and German attempts to outflank each other west of Paris and gain the upper hand before reaching the English Channel. Neither army succeeded, and September 1914 ushered in the era of trench warfare. The German failure greatly affected Moltke, who suffered a nervous breakdown in autumn 1914 and was removed as Chief of the German General Staff and replaced by General Erich von Falkenhayn. The first month of the Great War also brought huge causalities: about one million soldiers died or were wounded.

Perhaps the most well known image of World War I is of the filthy, hopeless, and ubiquitous trenches that would define the rest of the war and continue for another four years on the Western Front. Trenches ran in parallel lines: the first was the fire trench, or the frontlines; the second was the support trench, or reinforcements; and the third was the reserve trench, or supplies. Dr. Paul Mulvey of the London School of Economics notes, "A typical month was perhaps 4 days in the frontline, 4 in support, 8 in reserve and the remainder in rest, i.e. at barracks some miles from the front line."[23] The trenches were 6-8 feet deep and 5 feet wide. Nothing could

---

22. Chrystal, 2015.
23. Mulvey.

prepare a neophyte soldier for the horrors of the trenches although a piece of German propaganda in 1916 attempted: "Dig a trench shoulder-high in your garden: fill it half-full of water and get into it. Remain there for two or three days on an empty stomach. Furthermore, hire a lunatic to shoot at you with revolvers and machine guns at close range. This arrangement is quite equal to a war and will cost your country very much less."[24] This accurate description of the trenches, however, does not encapsulate their enormity. Strung all together, the trenches would nearly stretch across the circumference of the globe.[25]

24. Pitt, 1963.
25. Persico, 2004.

> **Did you know?**
>
> Despite the fact that Denmark was a neutral country, 30,000 Danes fought for Germany in World War I because Germany had annexed two Danish duchies in the nineteenth century and expected their inhabitants to fight. Many of these Danes hoped fighting would earn good will from Germany and allow their provinces to return to Denmark after the war. Thanks to Christian Urch, a history major and history buff, for this insight!

By October 1914, the "Race to the Sea" had ended with the First Battle of Ypres (October 19-November 22, 1914). Originally, the Germans had taken limited ground at great expense to both sides, but by November 8, German general Falkenhayn believed taking Ypres, known as "wipers" by the British, was impossible. Thus, the First Battle of Ypres was consider an Allied victory. As winter neared and soldiers began to realize they would not be going home for Christmas, there was one brief glimmer of light: the Christmas Day Truce of 1914, a celebration which would not happen during any other year of the war.

All throughout the Western Front on Christmas Day in 1914, cries of "Don't shoot! Don't shoot!" resounded through the trenches as enlisted men barreled over the sand bags into no-man's-land to exchange goods, including food or blankets, and sing carols like "Stille Nacht." The officers watched in horror as their men fraternized with the enemy. For one short day, German, British, and French commoners talked in no-man's-land about how they wanted the war to end. Many groups played soccer either with a real ball or some conglomeration of material they could scrap up. Some men even decorated Christmas trees. Those who experienced this truce marveled at the silence, repeating over and over "Not a shot was fired." They considered it the sanest part of the war. As December 26 arrived, shots began to fire, and the men scrambled back into the trenches. According to one German survivor, "Our Christmas was over. We took up again our old existence."[26] As the men started to arm themselves again, a young private realized he had left his cigars in no-man's-land; his comrades tried unsuccessfully to dissuade him unsuccessfully. Just as he popped his head over the trench, he was shot through the head and "part of his brains was sticking to my belt. . . . He was dead on the spot."[27] The example of this young man illustrates the hard realities of World War I in contrast to the all too brief Christmas Day respite.

While soldiers fought in horrific conditions on the ground in the dirty and foul trenches, the skies became home to a new class of fighter in 1915: the flying aces. Based on the French word 'l'as' used to depict Adolphe Pegoud, a high-scoring fighter pilot, "ace" became the word used to describe any pilot who shot down at least five enemy aircraft. Each country had its own heroes.[28] Britain's highest scoring pilot was Edward "Mick" Mannock who was credited with 73 victories, although some have disputed this number. He was killed over the Western Front in July 1918 and was posthumously

---

26. Richards, 1917.
27. Richards, 1917.
28. Clouting.

awarded the Victoria Cross. Georges Guynemer represented the French and also died on the Western Front in September 1917. Although he did not have the greatest number of kills for France — although Gynemer still had over 50 —, he was the most popular French ace during World War I. Perhaps the most famous ace from World War I, however, is Manfred von Richthofen of Germany, also known as the "Red Baron." Killed in action in April 1918, Richthofen, officially credited with at least 80 kills, still received a burial with full military honors from the British.

> **Fun Fact**
>
> Pilots have traditionally entered aircraft from the left side—yes, always the left side—is because of the original fighter pilots of World War I. Many pilots came from cavalry units, who mounted a horse on the left side to accommodate their sword, which was always carried on the left. Thanks to Lieutenant Colonel Gil Petrina (ret.) for this insight!

Thousands of miles away from the Western Front, the Middle Eastern theater of World War I witnessed the power of the moribund, or dying, Ottoman Turks. From April 22, 1915 to January 9, 1916, the Allies, predominantly the Australian and New Zealand Corps (ANZAC), fought the Gallipoli and Dardanelles campaign, part of a joint naval and land campaign seeking to capture Constantinople, which would allow Allied ships to pass through the Dardanelles and to cripple the Ottoman Empire, obligating the country to withdraw from the war. Although the naval component in February and March 1915 had failed, the Allies still went forward with the land element. The Turks overpowered the Allied forces and maintained the higher ground, and the Allies were unable to advance, leading to trench warfare just like in the Western Front. The troops finally had to evacuate in December 1915 and January 1916. While this campaign failed, it did slightly weaken the Ottomans, eventually forcing them to leave the war a couple months before Germany in 1918.

The failure of the Gallipoli and Dardanelles campaign brought major political ramifications for the British First Lord of the Admiralty, Winston Churchill. As one of the major figures who oversaw the campaign, Churchill received most of the blame for the massacre. He was removed from his Admiralty position, and Churchill avoided British politics for a little while, instead turning to painting. His wife, Clementine Churchill, later remembered that it was a challenging time for Winston: "I thought he would die of grief."[29] In addition to his art, Churchill also fought in World War I in Flanders from November 1915 to May 1916.[30] Churchill's time in the trenches certainly assisted him in understanding the perspective of the common soldier, which was of great use to him as Prime Minister during World War II.

---

29. Johnson, 2009.
30. Johnson, 2009.

> **Fun Fact**
>
> Mustafa Kemal, a prominent Turkish military leader in the Gallipoli campaign, helped expunge the Allies from Turkey. He later became the first president of the Republic of Turkey in 1923, greatly modernized and secularized the country, and adopted the name Ataturk, which means, "Father of the Turks."

As the ANZACs fought the Turks in the spring of 1915, the French and British continued to fight the Germans on the Western Front during the Second Battle of Ypres (April 22-May 25, 1915). This battle was notable for two reasons: it marked the beginning of chemical warfare and it inspired a poem that has endured for a century. Fritz Haber oversaw the German gas warfare program, and on April 22, 1915, the Germans first used chlorine gas, which was a noxious green cloud effective against unprotected soldiers. An estimated 1,100 soldiers were killed from gas at Ypres. Rudolph Binding, a German soldier who watched the fleeing Brits, observed, "Of course, the entire world will rage about it first and then imitate us," which was exactly what happened.[31] Six months later in October 1915, the Brits used gas at Loos, albeit somewhat unsuccessfully as it blew back in their face. Soldiers could protect themselves from these gas attacks relatively easily; the British opted for wet handkerchiefs while the French preferred urine-soaked rags. As technology developed, the gases became more lethal with the development of colorless and odorless phosgene and mustard gases. Soldiers eventually needed gas masks to protect against these new toxic fumes.

---

31. Binding, 1924.

Did you know?

When the Germans attempted to fire tear gas at the Russians at Warsaw in January 1915, it was so cold that the gas froze rather than vaporizing, thus saving the Russians from the horrible fate of a gas attack.

In addition to the impact of deadly gases, the Second Battle of Ypres also inspired Lieutenant Colonel John McRae to write the legendary poem, "In Flanders Fields," which has been studied and memorized by schoolchildren around the globe. McRae was a Canadian physician who fought on the Western Front and died of pneumonia in 1918. On May 2, 1915 during the Second Battle of Ypres, McRae's friend and former student, Lieutenant Alexis Helmer, was killed instantly when a six inch, high explosive canon shell burst nearby. This event deeply moved McRae, who, upon observing the poppies appearing around the graves and ditches, spent twenty minutes penning the fifteen-line poem. Sergeant Major Cyril Allinson came upon McRae as he finished writing, and McRae handed the verses to Allinson.

Reflecting back on that moment, Allinson observed, "The poem was an exact description of the scene in front of us both. He used the word blow in that line because the poppies actually were being blown that morning by a gentle east wind. It never occurred to me at that time that it would ever be published. It seemed to me just an exact description of the scene."[32]

World War I is perhaps best known for the battles that took place in 1916: Verdun, Jutland, and Somme. The Battle of Verdun lasted ten months (February 21-December 13, 1916), causing over half a million casualities from which both the Germans and the French never recovered. German General Falkenhayn had picked the ancient fortress city of Verdun, surrounded by small forts like Fort Douaumont, and wanted to kill as many Frenchmen as possible to force them to leave the war by bleeding them dry. Beginning on February 25, 1916, the Germans took Fort Douaumont, Verdun's most important fort at great cost. Kaiser Wilhelm II , however, insisted on German victory, making the battle especially costly. Scholars and military historians agree that the Germans should have called the attack off when it lessened in success. But they didn't know when to stop. Although not a decisive battle in the Great War, Verdun will be forever remembered "as the slaughterhouse of the world," in the words of an American ambulance driver visiting Verdun in 1917.[33] The French did not retake Fort Douaumont until October 1916.

---

32. Roland, 2011.
33. Jankowski, 2014.

Chapter 2: The Course of the Great War

In Flanders Fields

*In Flanders fields the poppies blow
Between the crosses, row on row
That mark our place; and in the sky
The larks, still bravely singing, fly
Scarce heard amid the guns below.
We are the Dead. Short days ago
We lived, felt dawn, saw sunset glow,
Loved and were loved, and now we lie
In Flanders fields.
Take up our quarrel with the foe:
To you from failing hands we throw
The torch; be yours to hold it high.
If ye break faith with us who die
We shall not sleep, though poppies grow
In Flanders fields.*

— John McCrae (1872-1918)

Around the same time, the British and Germans engaged in the largest naval battle of World War I, the Battle of Jutland (May 31-June 1, 1916), which included 250 ships and 100,000 men. The Germans had grown their navy and planned to ambush the British in the North Sea, but the British learned about the ambush from code breakers and arrived early. At first, the British fleet in the North Sea only consisted of David Beatty's battlecruisers. When two ships were lost and the flagship was damaged, the British withdrew until John Jellicoe's Grand Fleet arrived. Outgunned, the Germans turned toward home. Great Britain lost fourteen ships out of twenty-eight dreadnoughts and five battlecruisers while Germany lost eleven out of sixteen dreadnoughts and five battlecruisers. Although the battle was technically a tie, Britain controlled the High Seas after the Battle of Jutland, and Germany resorted to submarines.

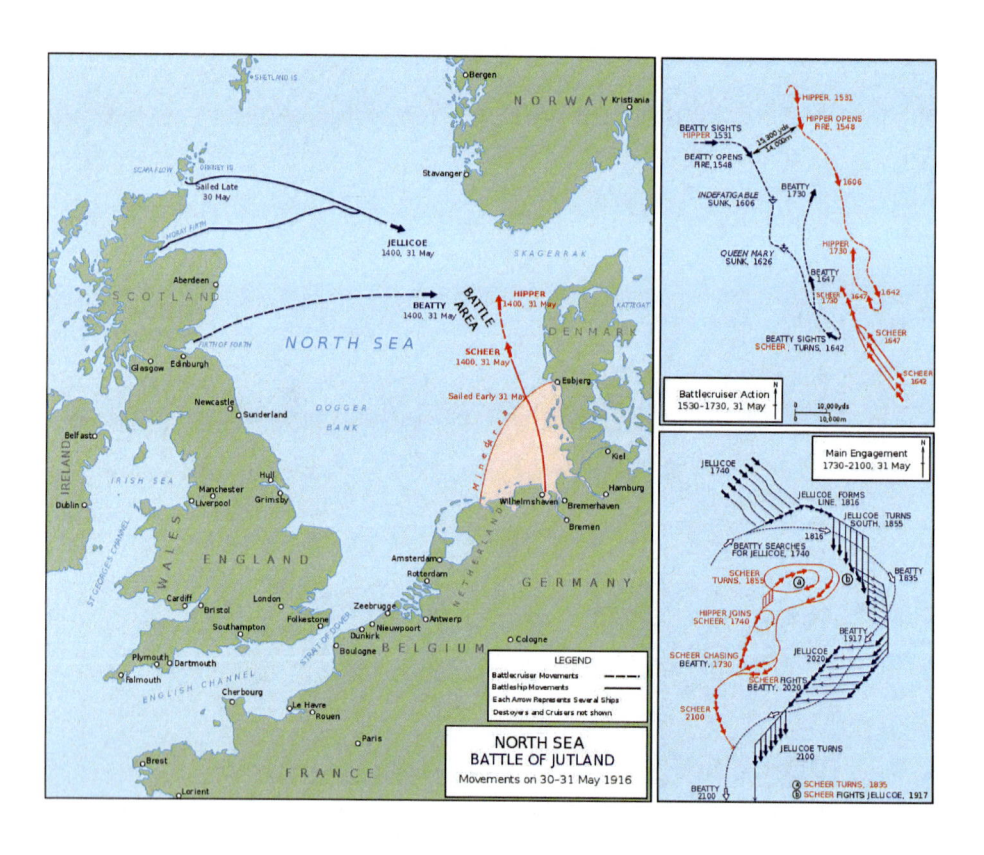

> **Did you know?**
>
> Winston Churchill, the First Lord of the Admiralty from 1911 to 1915 until the failure of the Dardanelles and Gallipoli campaigns, wrote about the Battle of Jutland in his 1924 work about the Great War, *The World Crisis*. Just four years later in 1928, Churchill impressively depicted this complex battle with wine glasses on the dining table (with the tablecloth removed!). According to a guest of the Churchills, James Lees-Milne, who was an undergraduate at Oxford, "Mr. Churchill spent a blissful two hours demonstrating with decanters and wine-glasses how the Battle of Jutland was fought. It was a thrilling experience. He was fascinating. He got worked up like a schoolboy, making barking noises in imitation of gunfire and blowing cigar smoke across the battle scene in imitation of gunsmoke."[34]

Just as the Germans had hoped bleed out the French and to force them to leave the war at Verdun, the Allies sought a decisive victory against Germany in a campaign at the Somme (July 1-November 18, 1916). At least, that's what British Field Marshal Haig thought. Since the Germans were putting a lot of pressure on the French at Verdun, the British would lead at the Somme. The British began with a 7-day bombardment, but they did not experience a quick breakthrough. They then rushed toward the German trenches, causing countless deaths. In some places, dead Brits covered the ground, the artillery had not cute the wire, making the rush over no-man's-land to the enemy German trenches challenging. Additionally, more Germans had survived the artillery 7-day bombardment than anticipated. Even so, when Germans like Musketier Karl Blenk saw the British advances, he felt sure they would overpower the German trenches. But they were only walking! According to Blenk, "If only they had run, they would have overwhelmed us."[35]

---

34. Gilbert, 1992.
35. Kershaw, 2016.

On the first day, 19,000 Brits died, making it the bloodiest day in British military history and the bloodiest day of both World War I and World War II. As historians Audoin-Rouzeau and Becker note, "*No* day in the Second World War was so deadly, even on the Eastern Front."[36] The battle itself was also quite bloody and slow; over the 141 days of the campaign, Britain advanced only seven miles. Marcel Savonnet, a French poilu or "shaggy one" who fought in Verdun, remembered the savagery of the battle: "It was butchery…Every day death rained down, every day more bodies…Today you can see the whole pattern of the war, the big picture, but we couldn't. Each soldier had his own little corner, his own narrow view of what was happening. We were isolated, and all we could think about was staying alive."[37]

---

36. Audoin-Rouzeau and Becker, 2002.
37. Kladstrup and Kladstrup, 2006.

> **Fun Fact**
>
> The first tanks appeared at the Battle of the Somme on September 12, 1916, thanks to the British. In fact, Winston Churchill, who was First Lord of the Admiralty from 1911-1915, championed this cause early in the war (1914), requisitioning Rolls-Royces covered in steel armor, which were the earliest version of the tank.[38] Some older generals, like British Field Marshal Haig, were skeptical of these iron elephants. Years later in 1925, Haig gave a speech at the Royal College of Veterinary Surgeons, which the *Times* of London described the next day: "He was all for using aeroplanes and tanks, but they were only accessories to the man and the horse, and he felt sure that as time went on they would find just as much use for the horse — the well-bred horse — as they had ever done in the past."[39] Others, including modern French historian Michel Goya, saw the introduction of tanks in 1916 as "a break, a turning point, the decisive pass from classic warfare to modern war."[40] Since Haig died in 1928, he never witnessed how wrong he was.

As the Allies fought the Germans in the famous battles of Verdun and the Somme, the Brusilov Offensive erupted on the Eastern Front in summer 1916. Also known as the "June Advance" (June 4-September 20, 1916), the Brusilov Offensive against the Austrians is perhaps the most famous campaign on the Eastern Front and was the most successful Russian offensive, in part, because it combined short artillery bursts and shock troops (troops especially trained for sudden attacks against an enemy). It also served to help relieve pressure from the Western Front during the Allied attack on the Somme. None of the Russian offensives that followed had the same success, which would later contribute to the Russian Revolution of 1917. Nonetheless, the triumph of the Brusilov Offensive caused Austria-Hungary to rely increasingly more on Germany.

---

38. Johnson, 2009.
39. *Times*, 1925.
40. Goya, 2004. "L'année 1916 marque une rupture, un tournant, le passage déterminant de la guerre classique à la guerre moderne."

As a result of the failure of Verdun, Field Marshal Paul von Hindenburg and his aide General Erich Ludendorff replaced Falkhenhayn on August 29, 1916. In September, Hindenburg and Ludendorff discussed the feasibility of and then began work on building a defensive system to keep the Allies out of Germany that was originally called the Siegfried Line. Later, in honor of the field marshal, the Allies called it the Hindenburg Line. It ran one hundred miles from Arras to Soissons and successfully protected against Allied offensives in 1917 with barbed wire and zigzagging trench lines.

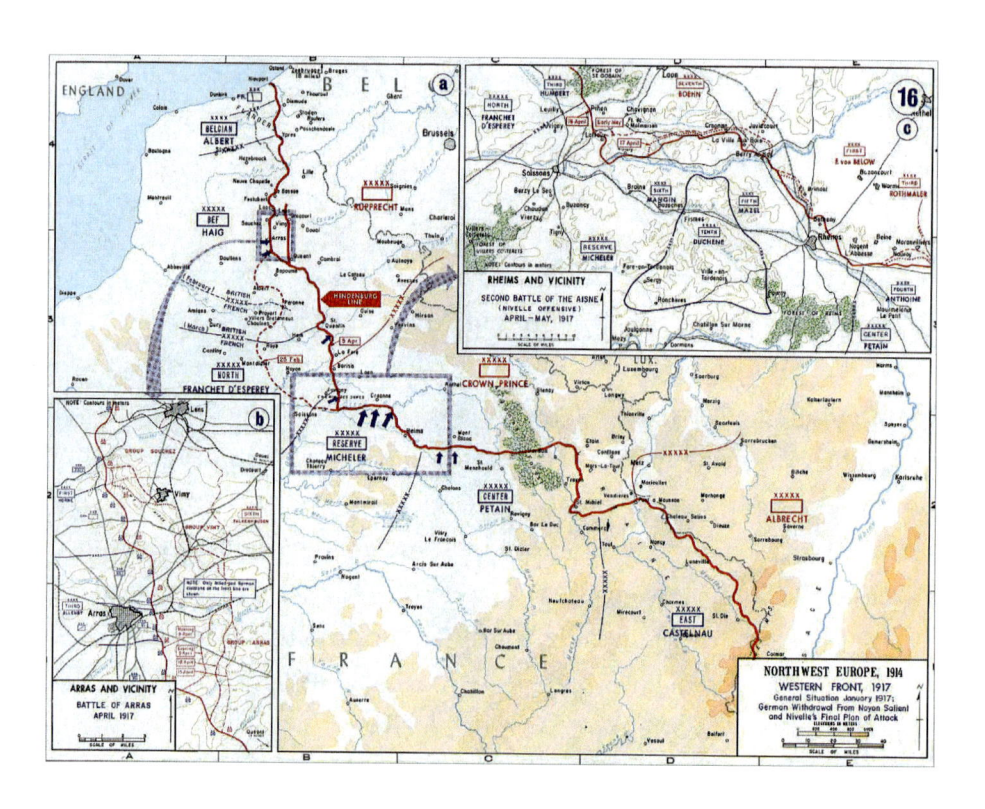

While the Germans began to build the Hindenburg Line, the Allies had already started a third battle at Ypres, known as the Battle of Passchendaele (July 31-November 10, 1917) due to the name of a prominent village nearby. After the failure at Jutland, the Germans had resorted to patrolling the seas with U-boats. British Field Marshal Douglas Haig believed an Allied offensive against the Germans in northern France that broke through the German lines could also lead to liberating the ports which housed submarines on the French coast near the English channel. The British began the attack with the Messines Ridge operation, which accomplished its objective. The recurring summer rain, however, made it challenging for the Allies. In September, the weather improved, only to turn back to rain. The Allies did effectively capture Passchendaele, but the railway that Haig had hoped to seize was still 5 miles away and untaken. In November 1917, the campaign was called off, and the Allies retreated in 1918, facing German offensives.. The battle had been futile, and countless men lost their lives.

Did you know?

With all the free time in the trenches in between attacks, many soldiers resorted to writing poetry, often depicting the horrors of battle. One such poem, "Dulce et Decorum Est," was written by Wilfred Owen, a British soldier killed in November 1918, and was published posthumously in 1920. "Dulce et decorum est pro patria mori" is a Latin phrase from Horace, the great Roman poet, glorifying dying for one's country, which roughly translates to "it is sweet and fitting to die for one's own country." Owen, however, did not see the splendor in dying for one's country; instead, he portrayed the gas attacks and the pain of the trenches.

America had entered the war on April 6, 1917 and began to send soldiers by the hundreds across the ocean to fight. The Germans knew they had to go on the offensive before they were inundated with fresh Americans eager to finish the war. Additionally, with Russia out of the war due to the Russian Revolution of 1917 and the Eastern Front no longer necessary, Germany could focus all its power on the Western Front. In 1918, General Ludendorff crafted a five spring and summer offensives called the *Kaiserschlacht*, or Kaiser's Battle, which included Operations Michael, Georgette, Blücher-Yorck, Gneisenau, and Marneschutz, to finish the war once and for all. The first offensive, Operation Michael (March 21-April 5, 1918), was extremely successful. Using gas and artillery, the Germans made gains in miles, an exceptionally uncommon feat during World War I. The Germans, however, only penetrated in some parts, which tended to be British lines, and the Allies managed to hold. As the offensives continued, they became more predictable, and the Germans never executed the fifth and final operation. Unfortunately, the tactical breakthrough and German victory Ludendorff sought eluded the Germans, and the German Spring Offensives largely failed.

Dulce et Decorum Est

BY WILFRED OWEN

Bent double, like old beggars under sacks,
Knock-kneed, coughing like hags, we cursed through sludge,
Till on the haunting flares we turned our backs,
And towards our distant rest began to trudge.
Men marched asleep. Many had lost their boots,
But limped on, blood-shod. All went lame; all blind;
Drunk with fatigue; deaf even to the hoots
Of gas-shells dropping softly behind.

Gas! GAS! Quick, boys! — An ecstasy of fumbling
Fitting the clumsy helmets just in time,
But someone still was yelling out and stumbling
And flound'ring like a man in fire or lime. —
Dim through the misty panes and thick green light,
As under a green sea, I saw him drowning.

In all my dreams before my helpless sight,
He plunges at me, guttering, choking, drowning.

If in some smothering dreams, you too could pace
Behind the wagon that we flung him in,
And watch the white eyes writhing in his face,
His hanging face, like a devil's sick of sin;
If you could hear, at every jolt, the blood
Come gargling from the froth-corrupted lungs,
Obscene as cancer, bitter as the cud
Of vile, incurable sores on innocent tongues, —
My friend, you would not tell with such high zest
To children ardent for some desperate glory,
The old Lie: *Dulce et decorum est*
Pro patria mori.

Notes:
Latin phrase is from the Roman poet Horace: "It is sweet and fitting to die for one's country."

> **Did you know?**
>
> At the Battle of Belleau Wood (June 1-26, 1918) during the German Spring Offensives, the United States Marine Corps first proved itself as more than simply a part of the Navy. Although the two divisions of Marines suffered greater losses on the single day of June 6, 1918 than any other day in their history, they did not back down. This battle is a touchstone for the Marine Corps and an important part of their history. The French renamed Belleau Wood after the battle "the Wood of the Marine Brigade," and lore says that the Germans referred to the Marines as *teufelhunden*, or devil dogs.

Although the Germans had originally succeeded in their offensives, the Allies' ability to maintain their positions weakened the Germans. By July 1918, the German strength had worn out, and the Allies began their own offensive, which became known as "Hundred Days" or "Advance to Victory" because it lasted roughly one hundred days — officially ninety-five — from the first major battle at Amiens (August 8-11, 1918) to the Armistice on November 11, 1918. The British Expeditionary Force gained seven miles on a single day, a feat unheard of during the war. After four days of this assault, its effect lessened. The Allies, however, had learned from previous years and previous errors and began offensives in other areas. In essence, the Allied offensives became coordinated hammer blows that turned out to be extremely efficacious. The Germans were pushed back to the lines of 1914, and, by November 1918, Germany could fight no more.

> **Fun Fact**
>
> Several military campaigns in history have been called the "Hundred Day" campaign, including the most famous: Napoleon's 100 Days in 1814.

As the Allied forces began offensives in the European front in the fall of 1918, the British led an offensive in the Sinai and Palestine Campaign, beginning with the Battle of Megiddo (Armageddon). This campaign would lead to the collapse of the Turks and their exit from the war. British General Allenby employed Allied deception to make the Turks think the Allied forces would come farther east and then crushed the Ottomans at Sharon and Nablus before any Turkish reinforcements or assistance could arrive. At Megiddo, Allenby and his forces utilized a coordinated attack of cavalry, infantry, artillery, and aircraft to defeat the Ottomans. Damascus, along with Beirut and Aleppo, fell on October 1, 1918. Faced with such devastating defeats, the Turks capitulated and signed a peace settlement with the Allies at Murdos on October 30, 1918. A 600-year-old empire had ended, and the Allies now controlled the Middle East.

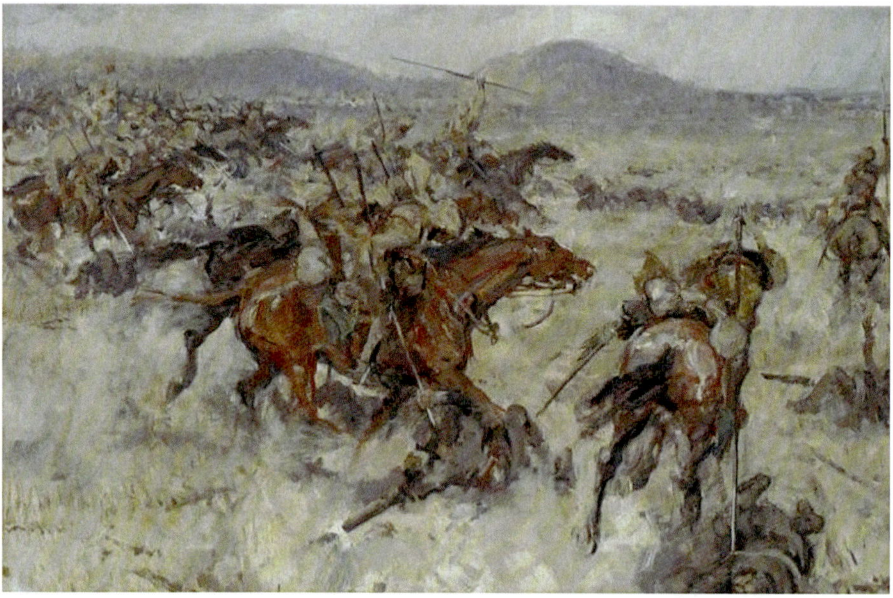

CHAPTER 3

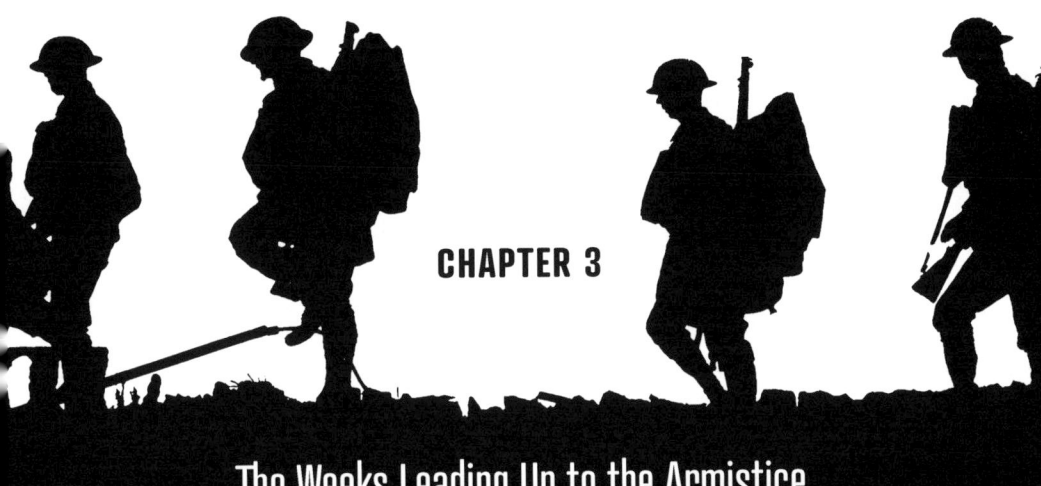

The Weeks Leading Up to the Armistice
October 30-November 10, 1918

"One Condition That Can Save the Hun"

In October and November 1918, the Central Powers began to collapse. The Turks left the war on October 30. Similarly, the Italians defeated the Austrians at Vittorio Veneto, a battle that took place from October 24 to November 3, 1918. After the Italian victory, Austria-Hungary asked for an armistice, which was signed and took effect on November 4, 1918. Thus, only the Germans remained as a prominent Central Power.

While the battles of late 1918 certainly claimed many lives, Spanish Influenza or La Grippe, which struck in the same year, was the greater killer. In fact, over a third of American soldiers who died perished from the flu. Ironically, the disease seemed to have a greater impact on younger, healthy people. The Spanish Influenza killed at least 20 million people although some scholars believe the causalities could be as high as 40 million. The impact was so severe that more people died in four months than in four years of fighting.

> **Fun Fact**
>
> The Spanish Influenza did not originate in Spain, but it got its name from the Spaniards being the first to report about the flu in the newspapers. Other governments were afraid of deflating public morale. Scholars believe that the single year of Spanish Influenza caused more deaths than four years of the Bubonic Plague in the Middle Ages.

Back on October 3, 1918, the Germans had asked for President Wilson's assistance in arranging an armistice with the Allied powers. Chancellor Georg van Hertling had resigned on September 30, 1918, and Prince Maxmilian of Baden, a relative of the king, was appointed to succeed Hertling. Prince Max began work in negotiating an armistice aware of the failing German government and military. Several abrupt and rapid political and military changes began to occur, further indicating the fiasco of the declining-in-power German monarchy. In late October, General Wilhelm Groener replaced Quartermaster General Ludendorff. A sailor's revolt in Wilhelmshaven took place on October 29-30, 1918, spurring rebellions all throughout Germany.

> **Did you know?**
>
> Before Woodrow Wilson became president of the United States, he was the president of Princeton and well known as an excellent professor. Wilson won the presidency by supporting isolationism and promising to stay out of the great European conflict. Nevertheless, he believed the United States could serve as a mediator between the European countries. A progressive, Wilson asked Congress for a declaration of war on April 2, 1917 to enter the Great War and "make the world safe for democracy." In January 1918, Wilson delivered his Fourteen Points, the last of which desired to create a League of Nations to guarantee political independence and territorial integrity. Many American citizens did not

> share Wilson's interest in uniting with other countries in the world, and the Senate voted against the Versailles Treaty, which included the League of Nations, by a small margin.

Americans knew that Germany was on its last leg, and many citizens and political leaders alike advocated for unconditional surrender. General Pershing advised the Supreme War council on October 30, 1918 for the unconditional surrender of Germany, explaining that otherwise the Germans would not understand and would simply begin fighting again at a later date if given an armistice. Former president Teddy Roosevelt, along with many Americans, agreed with Pershing. An October 14, 1918 newspaper article from the *Hartford Courant* included various statements from other U.S. newspapers that condemned President Wilson and urged for unconditional surrender — and, in some cases, killing Kaiser Wilhelm II. The Worchester Telegram was direct and desired surrender, but not the death of the Kaiser: "There is but one condition that can save the Hun from the grinding destruction of General Foch's terrible advance. That condition — an armistice."[41] While the others papers, ranging from the New York Times to the Chicago Tribune, may have couched their wording more carefully, all the papers agreed: the Allied forces under General Foch needed to gain the territory through conquest, not an armistice.

On November 4, 1918, the German government under Prince Max put out feelers to see if the Allies would even consider discussing an armistice with them. Despite the uncertainty of many citizens, political leaders, and generals in Allied countries, the Allies did agree on November 5 to converse with the Germans about armistice terms as well as reparation payments. Based

---
41. "Unconditional Surrender," 1918.

on this Allied response, the German government decided to negotiate an armistice with the Allies. The Germans sent a delegation that included a schoolteacher turned politician Matthias Erzberger, the head of the Catholic Center Party and the unenthusiastic leader of the armistice delegation, and midlevel representatives in the German military. No higher officials had been sent so that they did not have to face shaming from the German people. Even so, several years later, Adolf Hitler would condemn those sent to negotiate the German armistice as "November criminals."

> **Did you know?**
>
> Adolf Hitler frequently equated the "November criminals" who signed the Treaty of Versailles — the outcome of the armistice — with Jews and Marxists. Hitler (and other German nationalists) felt betrayed by Jews and Marxists, one of his main reasons for founding the Nazi-Socialist German Worker's Party in 1920. Additionally, since Erzberger was a politician and a civilian rather than a military commander, Hitler and others spread the "stab in the back" legend, namely the idea that the German military had not been defeated on the field, but politicians had negotiated a treaty when the military could have won. In reality, the German military was definitely demonstrating failures s in the field as well as being outgunned by the Americans.

On November 7, 1918, the German armistice group traveled as far as Tergnier, France, the most important railroad town in France about eighty miles from Paris. The trip began in automobiles and then transferred to a railway coach that once belonged to Napoleon III and featured a massive "N" indicating the ownership of the coach. Since Napoleon had ridden in this coach after the defeat of the French in the Franco-Prussian War of 1870-1871, the French certainly intended to communicate that the Germans were crushed and even more, that the French and other Allies had conquered them.

In the early morning of November 8, the train stopped forty miles from Paris in the Compiègne Forest. At 9 a.m., General Maxime Weygand, the

French aide to Marshal Ferdinand Foch, escorted the Germans to another railway coach labeled 2419D, a dining car that the French had turned into a conference room. Through an interpreter, Foch inquired about the mission of the Germans. Although the Germans had mostly conversed with President Wilson and the Americans about the possibility of discussing an armistice with the Allies, there were no United States representatives in the Compiègne Forest. The Germans replied that they understood that they had been sent to discuss armistice terms. Foch replied through the translator, "Tell these gentleman I have no proposals to make."[42]

Count Albert von Oberndorff, a French-speaking German, responded that they were there because of a message from President Wilson, which he began to read. The Germans desired that the armistice be based on Wilson's Fourteen Points, which upheld territorial integrity. Marshal Foch and the French — probably mostly due to the humiliation to which the Germans subjected the French after the Franco-Prussian War — had no intention of

---

42. Persico, 2004.

letting the Germans hide behind the Americans. For this reason, Foch interrupted Oberndorff's reading of Wilson's message and said that it must be the *Germans* seeking the armistice. Out of necessity, the Germans relented and indicated that they desired an armistice.

Thus prompted, French aide General Weygand began to deliver the Allied terms. The Germans would have to evacuate occupied lands, including Alsace-Lorraine, held by Germany since the Franco-Prussian War; the Allies would occupy Germany west of the Rhine River; the Germans would have to withdraw from Hungary, Romania, and Turkey; the Germans had to surrender ships, planes, weapons, trucks, and locomotives to the Allies; and the Allies would continue their naval blockade. In all, there were 34 conditions, including the first that indicated that the armistice would take effect six hours after signing and the last that noted the armistice would last 36 days with the possibility to renew.[43] The Germans would have 72 hours to contemplate the Allied provisions.

---

43. Rudin, 1944.

> **Did you know?**
>
> Alsace-Lorraine switched hands between France and Germany five times between 1845 and 1945. In many ways, the Alsatians have a duel identity that combines French and German heritages, although during the wars in the 1800s and 1900s, the Alsatians would frequently support one to oppose the other. Thus, during World War I, Alsace leaned toward France to protest Germany's stringent martial law and oppressive treatment of Alsatian soldiers and civilians: "[B]y 1914 French had come, in German-speaking Alsace, to be the badge of resistance to external tyranny, the language of Alsatian 'nationalism.'"[44]

Through German Army delegate General Detley von Winterfeldt, the Germans inquired whether hostilities would cease while the Germans deliberated and communicated Allied terms to the Kaiser and other German officials. Since roughly 2,000 men were killed each day, it was his attempt to save countless lives.[45] Again, the French remained unmoved. With orders from Prime Minister Clemenceau and his own unwillingness to relent, Foch refused.

> **Did you know?**
>
> Foch told his staff before the meeting with the Germans that he wanted "to pursue the *Feldgrauen* with a sword at their backs."[46] *Feldgrauen* is the German word for field gray, the color of the German military uniforms in the twentieth century. In other words, Foch wanted to use aggressive negotiations, rather than suspend hostilities, in order to coax Germany into officially surrendering. This is clear from Foch's plans for the future: the Allies had offensives planned extending into 1919![47]

---

44. Rudmose-Brown, 1915.
45. Persico, 2004.
46. Persico, 2004.
47. Persico, 2004.

By 11:30 a.m. on November 8, 1918, the Allies and German had completed discussing the armistice, and Marshal Foch gave Erzberger permission to radio the Kaiser at Spa. Extremely apologetic, Erzberger told the Kaiser that the armistice terms were very stringent and that he was sorry that he did not obtain a cease-fire. Due to the severity of the terms, Erzberger did not want to run the risk of the terms being leaked through the radio, so he sent the document via a twenty-two-year-old courier named Count Wolf-Heinrich von Helldorf and began writing "Observations on the Conditions of the Armistice with Germany," which discussed the hardships that the Germans would face under the Allied terms.

> **Fun Fact**
>
> Spa was a resort town in Belgium where the German High Command had its headquarters. In early November, the Kaiser fled there to avoid the riots and revolutions occurring all throughout Germany.

Count Helldorf left the Compiègne Forest with a French escort at 1 p.m. on November 8. Once they reached the German lines, Helldorf's party sounded cease-fire bugles and waved white flags, but with no success. The Germans refused to let their own men through because they believed that Helldorf and his escort were French. By nightfall, Helldorf had still been unable to pass through the German lines. The 72-hour time frame for the Kaiser and other leading German individuals to contemplate the Armistice was quickly streaming by. The clock was ticking.

In the meantime, the rest of the world thought that an Armistice had already been arranged. While Helldorf and his escort had unsuccessfully passed through the German lines, Field Marshal Foch had arranged for a local cease-fire for the German Armistice delegation to pass safely through the French lines. Foch had passed this information to the Germans at 2:30 a.m. on November 7 through a radio message transmitted from the Eiffel Tower.

The French intelligence — Deuxième Bureau — wrongly believed that a full-fledged armistice, rather than talks, would go into effect a half hour earlier. They passed the information to the American Embassy in Paris, which in turn reached Admiral Henry Wilson, an American naval commander in Brest.

When Admiral Wilson received the information of the supposed armistice, United Press journalist Roy W. Howard happened to be in Wilson's office. Wilson showed Howard the telegram, and, as a first-rate journalist realizing how much Americans would remember him if he first shared the news of the German armistice, Howard inquired, "Admiral, may I use that?" Admiral Wilson somewhat hesitantly assented. Thus, Howard passed the following wire to New York: "Paris, Nov. 7. – The Allies and Germany signed an armistice at 11 o'clock this morning. Hostilities ceased at 2 o'clock this afternoon." Howard's news was received with great rejoicing, and celebrations occurred in Brest, France, New York City, Washington, D.C., and various cities in England. Even small towns like Watertown, Wisconsin, thought that the armistice had been signed on November 7: "The city started celebrating, only to awaken the next morning to learn that the war had not ended, that it was still on but that it could, from all accounts, not last much longer."[48] Some soldiers even heard of the armistice, but figured it had to be a hoax because their commanders had not mentioned anything. For some reason, it took a while for the French and American governments to officially refute this false information. Eventually, both the French War Ministry and the American Secretary of State Robert Lansing issued denials that it was a permanent cease-fire and that an armistice had been reached.

---

48. Watertown *Daily Times*, 1952.

Did you know?

Roy Howard was a famous American newspaperman. Even when he earned a management role with E.W. Scripps Company, he still continued to work as a reporter. Although he was probably best known for the gaff about the World War I armistice, he also had a connection to a World War II figure. In March 1936, he interviewed Josef Stalin at the Kremlin.

Meanwhile on November 8 in the battlefield, both the French under Marshal Foch and the Americans under General Pershing wanted to retake Sedan, a city in northern France. Sedan held particular significance for the French because it was where Emperor Napoleon III and large numbers of his troops were captured during the Battle of Sedan (September 1-2, 1870), which decided the Franco-Prussian War in favor of the Germans. As a result, the Germans had held the city since 1870. Major General Hunter Liggett, who served under General Pershing, encouraged his superior to let the French take Sedan since it was extremely important to their honor.

Pershing did not concur. Instead, Pershing indicated that the 42nd and 77th divisions under Liggett, along with assistance from the 5th Corps and without observing traditional boundaries between units, would retake the city. 5th Corps commander Major General Charles Summerall decided to do more than "assist." He intended to send Brigadier General Frank Parker with parts of the 1st division to beat the 42nd and 77th to Sedan. Chaos ensued, and General Douglas MacArthur was temporarily arrested as a German spy. Liggett did not court-martial either Summerall or Parker because nothing disastrous had happened in their efforts to seek "glory." The Americans, however, did not have the honor or glory of retaking Sedan. That prestige went to the French. Supreme Allied Commander Foch sent Frenchmen to relieve the Americans as they seized the hills just before the city.[49]

---

49. Persico, 2004.

Like the Americans, Kaiser Wilhelm II was also thwarted from his plans of glory. Mutinies were taking place all over Germany. Some said that 10,000 Germans mutinied in Metz.[50] After the armistice was signed, the Kaiser planned to lead his armies back to Germany and restore order. The problem was that he had no army. Prince Max, Wilhelm's cousin who was serving as German chancellor, sent the Prussian minister of the interior, Herr Drews, to break this news to Kaiser Wilhelm. The king, however, as a descendent of Frederick the Great, had no intention of being pushed aside. He sternly retorted that he was not going to quit the throne "because of a few hundred Jews and a thousand workmen."[51]

> **Did you know?**
>
> Frederick the Great, who reigned from 1740 to 1786, was the longest ruling monarch in the Hohenzollern dynasty. He was known for promoting absolutism, bringing the Enlightenment to Prussia, reorganizing and strengthening the Prussian armies, increasing Prussian territories and making Prussia a military force to be reckoned with in Europe. Affectionately known as "Old Fritz," Frederick the Great was admired by Prussians — and Germans — for years to come.

Since the Kaiser refused to listen to Herr Drews, Prince Max called the king himself the evening of November 8 and urged Kaiser Wihelm to abdicate, using the familiar *du* form: "Your abdication has become necessary to save Germany from civil war and to fulfill your mission as a peacemaking emperor to the end."[52] Prince Max acknowledged that some Germans had unfairly blamed him for the riots and mutinies; nonetheless, that was what they believed. Again, the Kaiser refused to listen. Even if Max could not control the Bolsheviks and Jews, he could.

---

50. Persico, 2004.
51. Persico, 2004.
52. Persico, 2004.

The next morning at 10 a.m. on Saturday, November 9, General Groener, the successor to Hindenburg and Ludendorff, and General Hindenburg met the Kaiser to encourage him to abdicate since Wilhelm could no longer rely on the army to back him. Yet again, the Kaiser remained firm that he would stay in Spa, wait for the armistice, and lead his troops back to Germany. Groener repeated what Herr Drews and Prince Max had already said: the army no longer stood behind the Kaiser. This time, Kaiser Wilhelm agreed to take a poll of senior officers in the German army. If he did not have the support of the troops to put down the rebellion, he would abdicate. Some abstained, and of the twenty-four who replied, twenty-three said that he did not have the necessary backing. Only one officer said that the army would follow and assist the Kaiser.

With that, Kaiser Wilhelm II agreed to abdicate the Prussian throne, ending four hundred years of the Hohenzollern dynasty as the ruling house of Brandenburg-Prussia. To his surprise, he discovered that the message had already been sent! With information from Prince Max, the Wolf Telegraph Agency in Berlin had reported that the Kaiser had abdicated: "The Kaiser and King has resolved to renounce the throne."[53] Enraged, the Kaiser declared that Prince Max had committed treason, but the German senior officers remained quiet until Hindenburg said that the Kaiser should travel sixty miles to Holland. Thus, at 3:30 p.m. on November 9, 1918, Kaiser Wilhelm abdicated the German throne. Prince Max also resigned, turning over the chancellorship to Friedrich Ebert, the leader of the Social Democrats. The German monarchy had become a republic.

> **Fun Fact**
>
> The Social Democratic Party of Germany (SPD) is Germany's oldest political party and was founded in 1875 with the union of two worker's parties. At the beginning of World War I in 1914, it was the largest party in Germany, receiving more than one third of the national vote. The party split during World War I due to disagreements about Germany's role in the war. The right wing under Friedrich Ebert restored order in a way that Kaiser Wilhelm could not and ended the Soviet-inspired mutinies in Germany. The SPD greatly contributed to the creation of the Weimar Republic, which lasted from 1919 to 1933.

Early Sunday morning the Kaiser left for Holland. He was briefly stopped at the Holland border before an aide tracked down a Dutch official who let the Kaiser and his party pass into Holland. Although the Kaiser and his party were dressed in civilian clothes, they were recognized once they were across the border and greeted with calls of "Vive la France!"[54]

Since the Kaiser had abdicated and Prince Max had stepped down, the new provisional government under Friedrich Ebert now had to deal with the armistice. Count Helldorf, who had been delayed by German forces two

---

53. Persico, 2004.
54. Persico, 2004.

days prior because they did not believe that he was a German messenger, finally made it through. With sixteen hours remaining on the armistice deliberation time, the new government sent a message that the French intercepted which stated that Erzberger and the German armistice delegation could sign the armistice. Erzberger himself received a message from Hindenburg about the armistice, indicating that the former should sign the armistice but still try to receive as many concessions as possible. Thus, with fifteen hours remaining on Foch's original deadline, the Germans had official approval to sign the armistice.

> **Did you know?**
>
> In January 1919, Germany held free elections and elected Friedrich Ebert as president of the Weimar Republic, which lasted from 1919 to 1933. The government was called the Weimer Republic because it established itself in Weimar, a town in central Germany, rather than in Berlin.

Nonetheless, Erzberger was intent on getting some concessions from the Allies. Several hours after the official approval at 8:30 p.m. on Sunday, November 10, the German armistice delegation was taken to Foch's car at 2:10 a.m. on Monday, November 11 to discuss the armistice terms. After three hours of discussion, the Germans received only two dispensations. Since the Germans possessed fewer than 1,700 planes, they did not have to turn over the 2,000 stipulated in the armistice terms.[55] The Allies would also consider the provisioning of Germany since Erzberger mentioned that it was hurting citizens.

---

55. Persico, 2004.

> **Did you know?**
>
> The Germans under Otto von Bismarck gave the French a fairly strict armistice after the Franco-Prussian War of 1870-1871. The French had to relinquish Alsace-Lorraine and pay a "war indemnity of five billion francs, the equivalent of $15 billion today."[56] Although some have blamed the French for their harsh armistice treaty toward Germany after World War I, they certainly had reason to be upset with Germany as France's indemnity and war costs of the Franco-Prussian War nearly bankrupted the country in the 1920s.[57] Regions that especially suffered were often wine-making areas, including Champagne where the sparkly, bubbly drink that we know today was first invented.

---

56. Kladstrup and Kladstrup, 2006.
57. Kladstrup and Kladstrup, 2006.

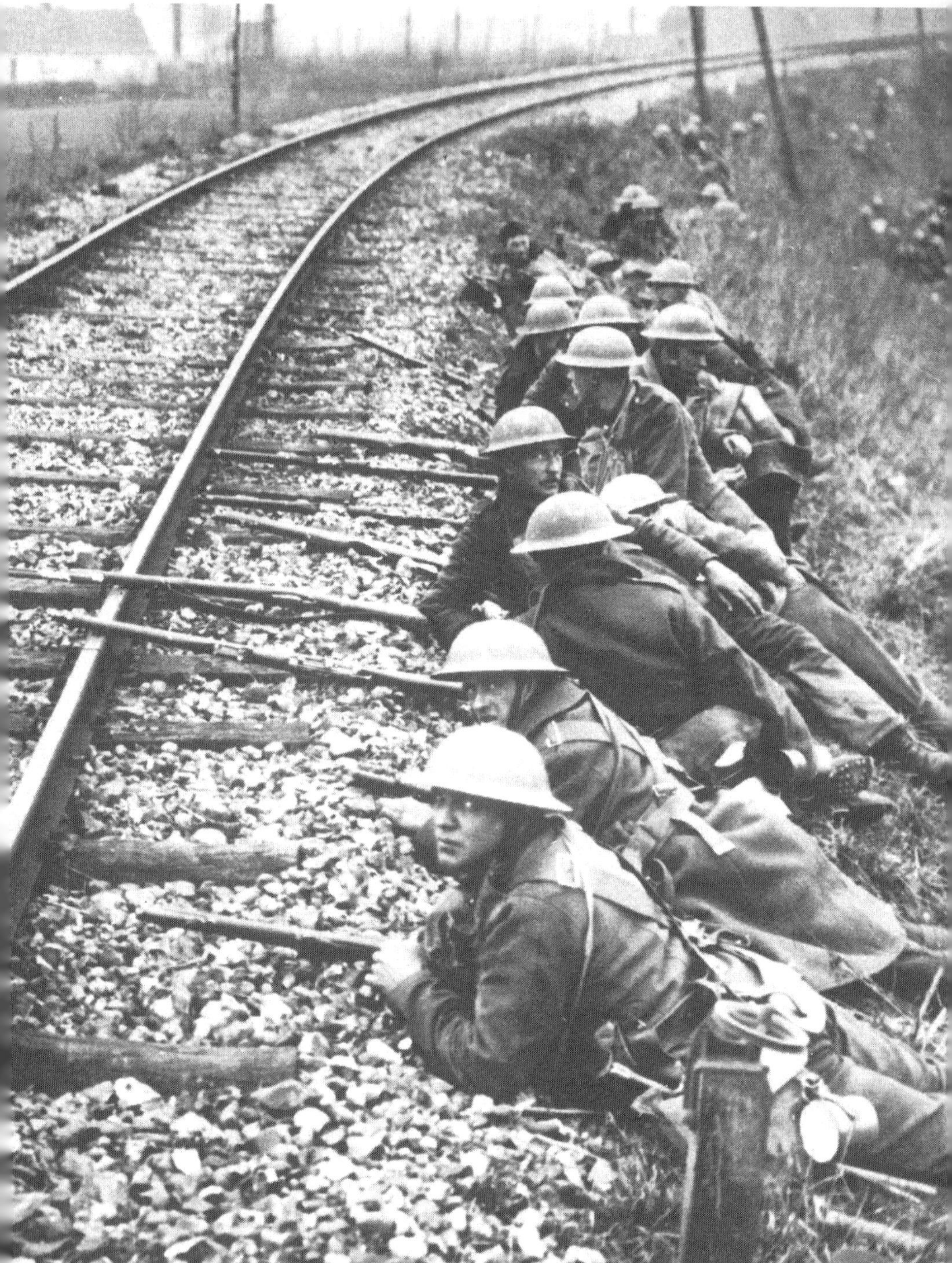

CHAPTER 4

Signing the Armistice
November 11, 1918 at 5:12 a.m.

"Hostilities Will Cease"

At 5:10 a.m., the Allies and Germans had agreed upon the armistice terms with two slight modifications. Marshal Foch and the British representative First Sea Lord Sir Rosslyn Wemyss signed the final draft of the armistice first and then the German delegation followed. It was 5:12 a.m. It would take effect six hours after it was signed. The official signing was moved back to 5:00 a.m. so that hostilities would cease at the deadline Foch had given for deliberation of the armistice: the eleventh hour of the eleventh day of the eleventh month.

Foch left the dining car at 5:30 a.m. and sent word to all commanders via telephone and radio, including from the Eiffel Tower, that the armistice had been signed and that fighting would end at 11:00 a.m. The cease-fire telegram said, "Hostilities will cease on the entire front beginning at 11:00

A.M. November 11. The Allied troops will not pass the line reached at that date and at that hour without a new order."[58]

```
              SIGNAL CORPS, UNITED STATES ARMY
                         TELEGRAM

         RECEIVED AT       EIFFEL TOWER RADIO TO ALL STATIONS
                              (5:30 AM.    Nov. 11, 1918)

   FROM MARSHALL FOCH TO COMMANDER-IN-CHIEF,

   1.  THE HOSTILITIES WILL BE STOPPED ON THE ENTIRE FRONT BEGINNING
       NOV. 11TH AT ELEVEN O'CLOCK. (FRENCH TIME).

   2.  THE ALLIED TROOPS SHALL NOT GO BEYOND THE POINT REACHED ON
       THAT DATE AND ON THAT HOUR UNTIL FURTHER NOTICE.

                    (SIG)      MARSHALL FOCH.

              EIFFEL TOWER RADIO TO GERMAN RADIO

   GERMAN PLENIPOTENTIARIES TO GERMAN HIGH COMMAND FOR COMMUNI-
   CATION TO ALL THE AUTHORITIES CONCERNED.

   ARMISTICE HAS BEEN SIGNED AT 5:00 A M THIS MORNING (FRENCH TIME)
   EFFECTIVE AT ELEVEN O'CLOCK THIS MORNING (FRENCH TIME) DELAY OF
   THE EVACUATION EXTENDED 24 HOURS FROM THE LEFT BANK OF THE RHINE.
   IN ADDITION TO THE FIVE DAYS THIS THIRTY ONE DAYS IN TOTAL. MODI-
   FICATION OF THE TEXT COMPARED WITH THE TEXT BROUGHT BY HALDORF
   WILL BE TRANSMITTED BY RADIO.

                    (SIG)      ERZBERGER.
```

While the armistice brought peace, it was only temporary and was only the beginning of peace negotiations between the Allies and Germans. Every thirty days, the armistice could either be renewed or allowed to lapse and fighting would begin anew. Additionally, if the Germans violated any portion of the armistice, fighting would resume with forty-eight hours notice. The Treaty of Versailles, signed six months later, would officially and finally end the war.

The Allies crafted the armistice with the intention of weakening the Germans so that it would be practically impossible for them to renew fighting.

---

58. Persico, 2004.

Some Allied leaders believed that the Germans were only seeking an armistice as a military move and that the Germans were intending to reform and regroup to bring about an eventual German victory. The Germans, however, did not have that intention; the strength of the military and the government was in rapid decline and only an armistice — and later a treaty — would bring about peace to the war-torn and devastated country.

> **Fun Fact**
>
> The railway carriage in which the Germans signed the armistice on November 11, 1918 was preserved and kept in the Compiègne Forest to commemorate the French victory in World War I. When the French fell after a short fight to the Germans in the summer of 1940, Adolf Hitler, Foreign Minister Joachim von Ribbentrop, and Luftwaffe Chief Hermann Göring watched the French representatives sign their armistice and much of their land to the Nazis on June 22, 1940.

The various leading generals had different responses to the armistice. German General Groener, Ludendorff's successor, messaged German troops in the West to maintain order among the men and forbid fraternization with the enemy. American General John Pershing was displeased when he received the message from the Eiffel Tower at 5:45 a.m. He wanted to continue fighting the Germans until they were defeated on the field. Three days later on November 14, the Allies had planned an offensive on Metz. Pershing pointed to a map on the wall of his staff room: "what an enormous difference a few more days would have made."[59] Marshal Foch himself had not even withdrawn an order from November 9 and instead encouraged the advance to speed up. In a similar vein, British Field Marshal Haig told his troops to stand fast, not where they were, but where they might be.

---

59. Persico, 2004.

> **Did you know?**
>
> The signing of the armistice benefited an unlikely group of people: librarians. The American Library Association had sent some books over during the war, but with a greater number of servicemen now stationed in Europe waiting to return home with nothing to do, sending books became a higher priority. The War Service Committee noted, "The signing of the armistice on November 11, 1918 brought fresh demands and opportunities and opened the way for a work which in volume and extent exceeded previous efforts."[60]

---

60. American Library Association Archives, 2012.

CHAPTER 5

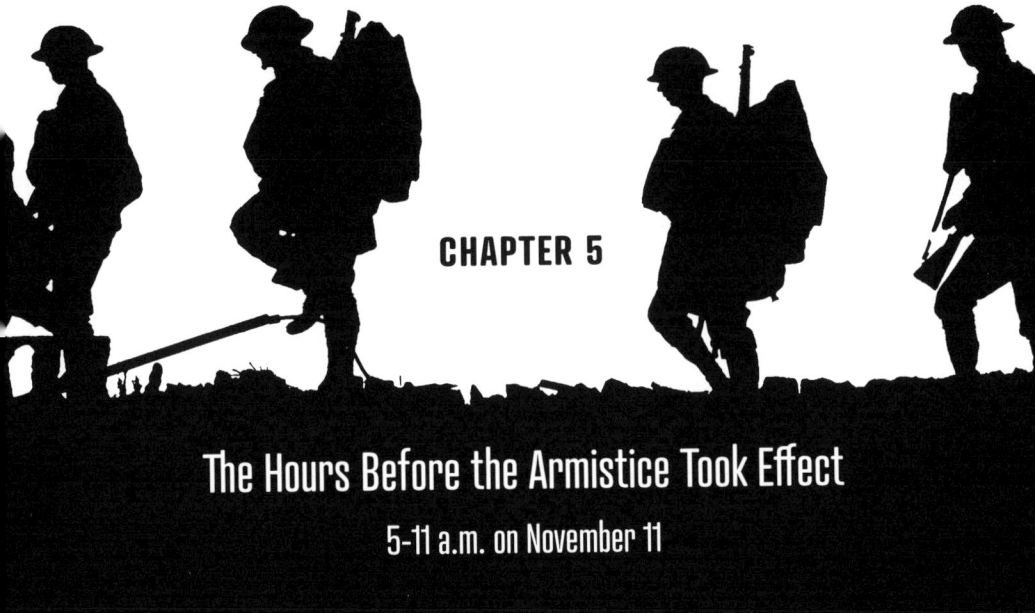

The Hours Before the Armistice Took Effect
5-11 a.m. on November 11

"The Crack of the Last Guns"

As high officers began to receive news of the impending armistice and cease-fire, many senior officers like Pershing passed on the message to cease hostilities at 11 a.m., but did not give any other instructions. This lack of direction left commanders of small units two options: continue fighting for professional honor and glory or save lives and risk professional ramifications.

Robert Cude, an ordinary Briton fighting for his country, wrote one sentence on the morning of November 11 that is almost certainly indicative of all the soldiers, no matter what side they were on: "If only I can last out the remainder of the time, and this is everyone's prayer."[61] While some commanders were seeking professional advancement, most men were hoping to make it out alive.

---

61. Persico, 2004.

Tragically, some men who had managed to survive almost four years of the war died in the war's last hour. Jim Fox of the Durham Light Infantry recalled how one of his sergeants died in the last hour of the war. From 6 a.m. until 11 a.m. as they waited for the armistice hour to arrive, the Germans and Americans exchanged an occasional shell. At 10 a.m., some shrapnel hit the sergeant: "Thought that was very unlucky. To think he'd served since 1915, three years until 1918, nearly four years and then to be killed within an hour of armistice…"[62]

The responses of commanders varied widely. Four American generals in particular responded differently to the news. Some men like Major Handford "Jack" MacNider refused to sustain any more casualties and were willing to risk disciplinary action to save the lives of their men. As his 2,000-man battalion crossed the Meuse near Mouzay, France, they observed that the Germans were directing a lot of machine gun fire in that direction. After the first couple men who attempted to cross piled at the bridgehead, MacNider decided to withdraw his men and did not receive any disciplinary action.[63]

> **Did you know?**
>
> Major MacNider did not suffer any harmful results for his decision. In fact, MacNider became quite a prominent officer and citizen. He helped found the American Legion and became National Commander in 1922, served as Assistant Secretary of War under President Calvin Coolidge, unsuccessfully ran for president in the 1930s, commanded the 158th Regimental Combat Team, also known as the Bushmasters (the author's grandfather fought in this unit) during World War II, and was promoted to Lieutenant General in 1951.

---

62. "Podcast 47: Armistice."
63. Persico, 2004.

General Liggett of the First United States Army, however, had a different response to crossing the Meuse. The 2nd, 89th, and 90th divisions suffered over 1,000 causalities with almost 800 seriously wounded and over 100 dead. Liggett stated that the crossing was necessary due to the Metz Offensive that would take place on November 14: "This offensive would have cut the German Army in two."[64] Due to the armistice, the Metz offensive was not necessary as the Germans gave up the ground willingly as opposed to the Allied forces needing to retake it.

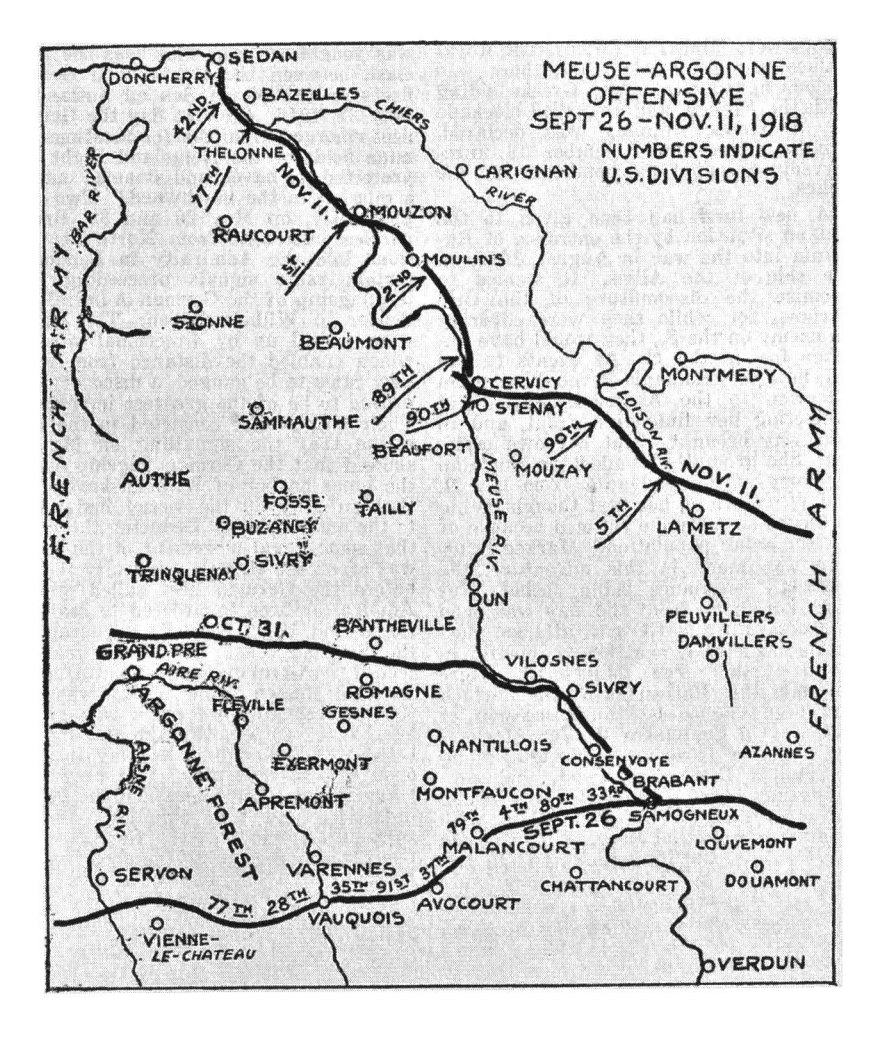

---

64. Persico, 2004.

> **Fun Fact**
>
> In Mouzay, which is located in northern France, World War I greatly influenced the community. The Americans who liberated the town discovered, to their surprise, that the children spoke German better than French. When they inquired why, the Americans discovered that the Germans had occupied Mouzay for the entire four years of the war.[65]

Major General Bunker Haan made a decision similar to Major MacNider: he called off the attack. Major General Haan, however, was already over the Meuse and had orders to go over the top and advance seven miles. When he called off the attack, the Germans kept shooting. He counted the German shots, which turned out to be 17 to 20 per minute, and told his men to fire 10 shots for every German shell. Soon the German shelling stopped, as did the American shelling.[66]

By contrast, General Robert Lee Bullard of the Second U.S. Army responded more like General Liggett. When Bullard received Foch's message from Pershing, he delivered the message that the armistice was to take effect at 11 a.m. without elaboration, leaving his men to choose whether to fight. Bullard himself believed that the Allies should continue fighting until 11 a.m. as his actions reveal: "I regarded this fighting as the last day of the war, so I went early, with an aide, to the front, to see the last of it, to hear the crack of the last guns in the greatest war of all ages."[67]

---

65. Persico, 2004.
66. Persico, 2004.
67. Persico, 2004.

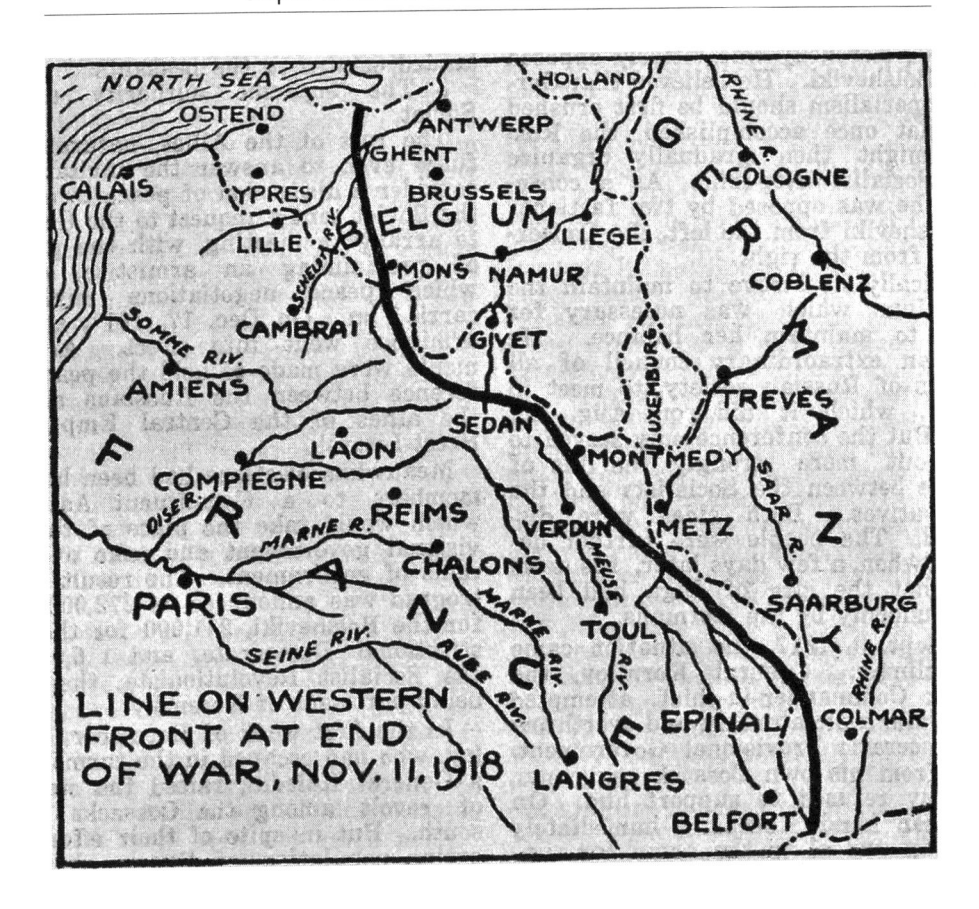

Chapter 5: The Hours Before the Armistice Took Effect

[Map: Line on Western Front at End of War, Nov. 11, 1918]

Sixteen American divisions were engaged on the Western Front, and the commanders were split somewhat evenly on how to proceed with the armistice notice. Seven decided to halt the attacks and did not continue any further; nine continued until the very last second of the war.[68]

While some American commanders fought on for prestige, many British and French commanders and units wanted to regain lost ground from early in the war, thereby restoring lost honor.

For the British Empire, that city was Mons, a devastating loss from August 1914. As the Canadian 42nd battalion rushed to reclaim the Belgian city,

---

68. Persico, 2004.

they came across the bodies of three men on a bridge into the city. All three were from the London Rifle Brigade and all had the Mons Star, which means they had fought in the 1914 Mons retreat only to die near Mons four years later in an effort to retake the city.[69]

The 5th Irish Lancers, who had similarly been driven from Mons in 1914, went through Mons and went to seize the high ground outside of the city at Saint-Denis to ensure that the Germans did not retake the city before 11 a.m.[70] They arrived just in time to see the Germans fleeing. The Canadian 2nd and 3rd divisions also reentered Mons and were warmly welcomed by the inhabitants.

---

69. Persico, 2004.
70. Persico, 2004.

Mons was clearly a symbol for the British Empire, but of what? In some respects, it brought closure to the British imperial troops who had retreated four years ago and finally were able to retake the city. On the other hand, it was an image of futility. For four years, war had divided Europe, and no substantial gains had occurred. The British, French, and Germans were simply back where they started, except with over eight million deaths and almost 30 million wounded.

Fighting continued up until 11:00 a.m. on the dot. Some men were gung-ho to say that they had fired the final shot of the Great War. The 26th Yankee division of New Englanders had a unique solution. The commanders allowed the men to tie ropes to guns and more than 200 doughboys grabbed the rope at 11 a.m. per the order of their commander, allowing all of them to say that they had fired the final shot of the war.[71]

As the time drew closer to 11 a.m., many men hunkered down, hoping to last just a few more minutes, or even seconds, until the fateful hour. For some, that was not to be, and they will be forever remembered as the final casualties of the war. The last Briton casualty was named Private George Edwin Ellison and had served in the military before the start of the Great War. As a member of the 5th Irish Lancers, he was part of the British Expeditionary Force that retreated. At 9:30 a.m. as he was scouting outside Mons for Germans, he was shot.

> **Did you know?**
>
> Private Ellison was later buried in a cemetery close to the putative first British causality of the war, Private John Parr, who was a seventeen-year-old messenger shot off a bicycle and killed on August 21, 1914.[72] Jon Cooksey, who has studied troop movements and war diaries on both sides for the Battle of Mons, notes that Parr and his comrade should not

---

71. Persico, 2004.

> have encountered enemy soldiers: "On 21 August, according to the battalion war diary, John Parr's regiment was 11 miles south of the position it would take up to fight at Mons — German units did not cross the Mons-Conde Canal until the afternoon of 23 August [1914]."[73] This evidence suggests that Private Parr either died during the Battle of Mons on August 23 (as his burial place by the Germans might suggest) or by friendly fire either from Belgians, French, or even British soldiers. If the former is true, then Parr may not have been the first British causality of the war.

The last French causality, Augustin Trébuchon, was the bearer of good news: troops by the River Meuse would receive soup at 11:30 a.m. after the cease-fire. As he went to deliver the message, the 40-year-old was shot and killed at 10:45 a.m.[74] Interestingly, Trebuchon's grave, along with the graves of the other French soldiers who died on November 11, gives October 11, 1918 as the death date. According to Hayes-Fisher, "It is said that after the war France was so ashamed that men would die on the final day that they had all the graves backdated."[75]

The last Canadian causality, Private George Lawrence Price, was much younger than the other two; he was only 25-years-old. Just north of Mons, Private Price and others were trailing retreating German and engaging in street fighting. As Price stepped outside from a house, a German sniper killed him at 10:58 a.m., a mere two minutes before the armistice took effect.

---

72. Persico, 2004.
73. Clare, 2014.
74. Hayes-Fisher, 2008.
75. Hayes-Fisher, 2008.

Chapter 5: The Hours Before the Armistice Took Effect

Private Henry Gunther of Baltimore, who had German ancestry, was not only the last American causality but also the final soldier to be killed in action on the Western Front. Earlier Private Gunther had lost his sergeant stripes for writing a letter home to a friend encouraging him to avoid the draft. When the Army censors intercepted the letter, Gunther was demoted. Just a minute before the armistice was to take effect, Gunther started firing at nearby Germans, who tried to wave him off. When Gunther began to rush them, despite the requests of his friend Sergeant Powell, the Germans returned fire and shot Gunther in the left temple. The time was 10:59 a.m.

Finally, after over four years of hard fighting, it reached 11 a.m. Those who survived breathed a sigh of relief. The U.S. Army Signal Corps put together a graphic record that illustrated the stark difference one minute can make. Three seconds before 11 a.m. show intense artillery activity, due to the irregularities. By contrast, three seconds after 11 a.m. are mostly still with two small aberrations, perhaps due to an exuberant doughboy firing a gun celebrating the end of the war. One minute before the hour all guns were firing at the River Moselle, but one minute after, all guns were silent. As Ben Cosgrove noted in a *Time* article, "No single picture can possibly capture the scope and the import of that instant, when four years of mechanized carnage came to an abrupt, long-dreamt-of end."[76]

For roughly 2,700 men on all sides, however, they lost their lives in these last six hours from when the armistice was signed until when it took effect, and an additional 8,000 men were wounded. As a point of comparison, during Operation Overlord (D-Day), Allied casualties (both wounded and killed) have been estimated at 10,000. If German casualties are included, another 4,000 to 9,000 men were killed.[77] Thus, the number of casualties

---

76. Cosgrove, 2014.
77. D-Day Museum, 2015.

during the six hours after the armistice was signed but before it took effect was on par with the number of casualties from D-Day.

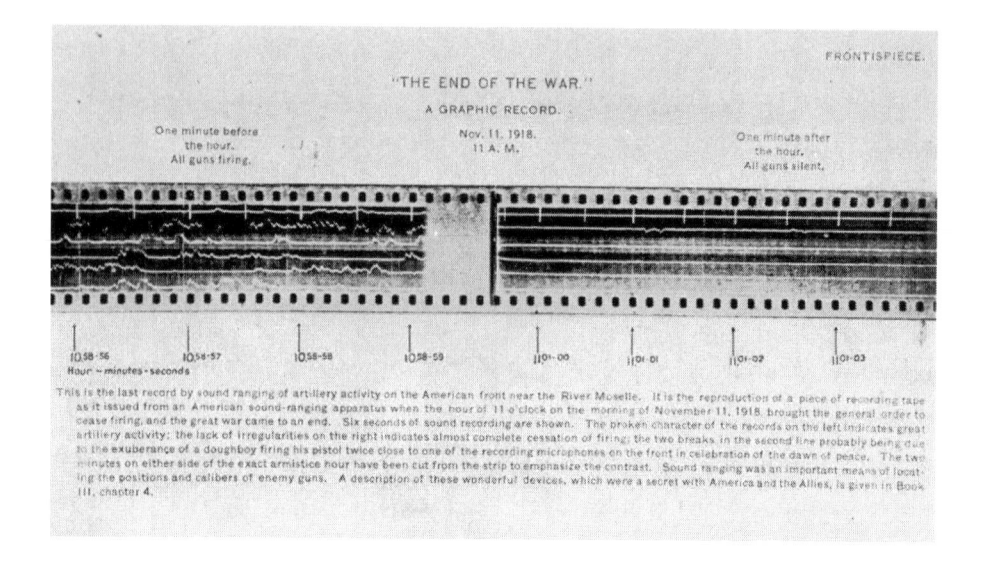

> FRONTISPIECE.
> "THE END OF THE WAR."
> A GRAPHIC RECORD.
> Nov. 11, 1918.
> 11 A. M.
> One minute before the hour. All guns firing.
> One minute after the hour. All guns silent.
>
> This is the last record by sound ranging of artillery activity on the American front near the River Moselle. It is the reproduction of a piece of recording tape as it issued from an American sound-ranging apparatus when the hour of 11 o'clock on the morning of November 11, 1918, brought the general order to cease firing, and the great war came to an end. Six seconds of sound recording are shown. The broken character of the records on the left indicates great artillery activity; the lack of irregularities on the right indicates almost complete cessation of firing; the two breaks in the second line probably being due to the exuberance of a doughboy firing his pistol twice close to one of the recording microphones on the front in celebration of the dawn of peace. The two minutes on either side of the exact armistice hour have been cut from the strip to emphasize the contrast. Sound ranging was an important means of locating the positions and calibers of enemy guns. A description of these wonderful devices, which were a secret with America and the Allies, is given in Book III, chapter 4.

Even so, some regiments did not receive the news of the armistice before 11 a.m. and continued fighting, suffering casualties. At 4:15 p.m. on November 11, over five hours after the armistice took effect, the forward elements of the 2nd Division received the last order to cease fire.[78]

The last deaths on the Western Front, however, did not occur until midnight on November 12. Retreating Germans thought they were the last to leave Hamont, a Belgian town, so they mined the railroad station. Tragically, one last train with German soldiers was just about to arrive from Antwerp. The explosion sent the car up in the air and killed hundreds of Germans thirteen hours after the armistice took effect.[79]

The men on the African front, however, got the last word as the final battle of World War I occurred between British and German troops in Northern

---

78. Persico, 2004.
79. Persico, 2004.

Rhodesia on November 12, 1918 because they had not received news of the armistice earlier. Additionally, the last German to surrender was Paul Emil von Lettow-Vorbeck, known as the African Hindenburg, on November 23, 1918 in German East Africa.

The fighting that took place in the six hours before the armistice took effect has puzzled individuals for a century. In 1920, the U.S. House of Representatives began an investigation to see why the men continued to fight until 11 a.m. A subcommittee thought that it would needless slaughter that some commanders persisted in attacking until the very last moment, but some House members thought that it was unfair to the wartime leaders since they had actually been on the battlefield and experienced death, filth, and sorrow like no one else. Therefore, the investigation found that no one was culpable for the November 11 bloodshed.

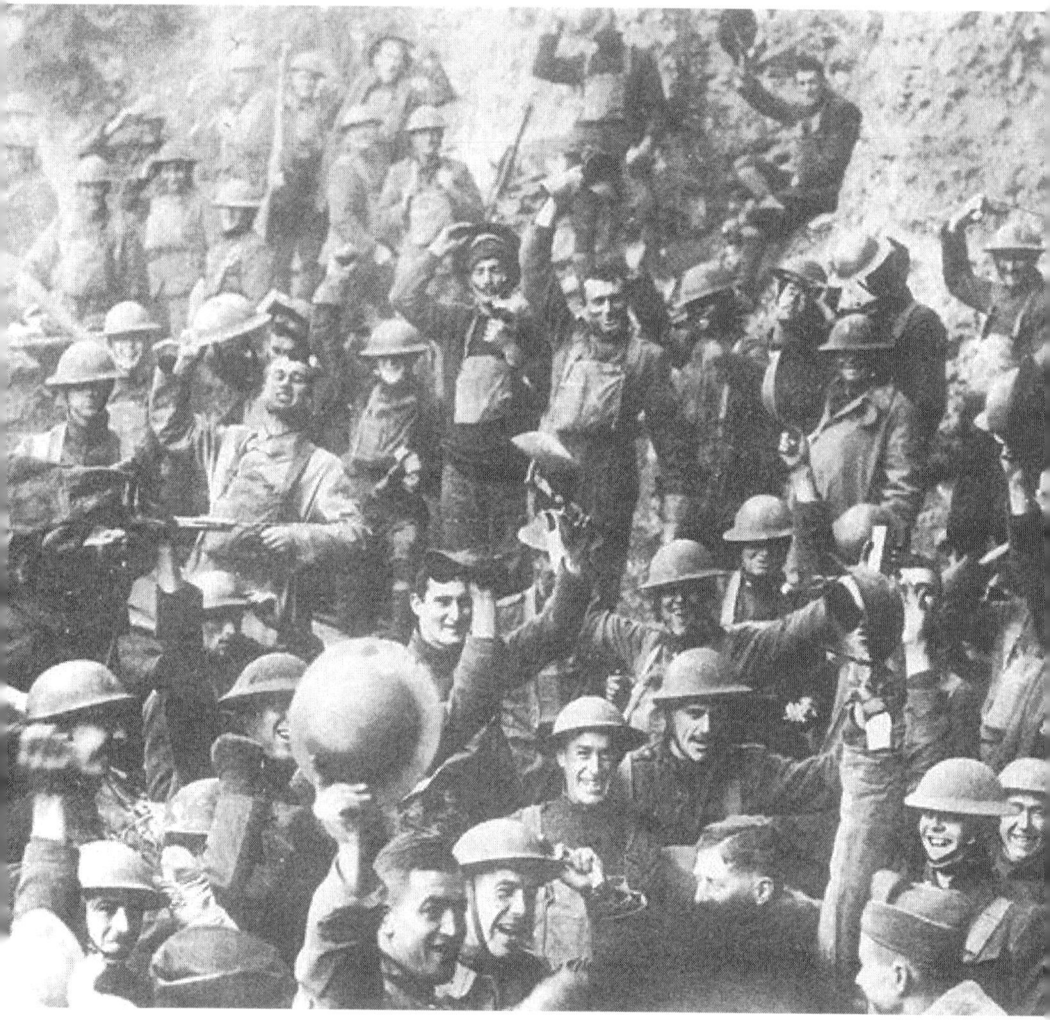

CHAPTER 6

Individual Responses to the Armistice

"A Quietness We Had Never Known"

On the battlefield, 11 A.M. ushered in a new dynamic for the soldiers, Allied or German: silence. For those soldiers who had not been told by their commanders that an armistice had been signed, they knew something was different when at 11 a.m., there was no artillery fighting, no brass flying, and no orders to go over the top. It was strangely still.

Then the field erupted with cries of "The war is over!" "Finie la guerre!" and "Der Krieg ist über!" It took a couple minutes for this truth to set in. Some soldiers were dumbfounded; others rejoiced with their comrades that they had survived. Still others prayed and thanked God.

Soldiers from different American divisions recounted the moments after 11 a.m. According to Connell Albertine of the 26th Yankee Division, "We then, being very excited, started shouting and hugging and kissing each other. We ran into no-man's-land and stood there, stunned by the quiet, a quietness we had never known."[80] Another in the 42nd Division remembered, "We didn't know what to do first, to cheer or to pray. I guess we really did both in the same breath."[81] F.C. Reynolds of the 29th Division described how, at first, the soldiers were quiet as they were extremely grateful to have survived and then their rejoicing turned more raucous: running in the street and yelling. According to Reynolds, "You can imagine — no, you can't imagine, it is impossible for anyone to imagine who did not experience it, the sense of relief and pure joy that came in our hearts."[82] Veteran Andrew Johnson recalled, "Armistice Day found us before Metz [a town in northeastern France]. We were waiting to storm a great walled city which would have cost us many men, as we would have to cross a level plain about two miles long."[83] Thus, for the everyday soldier, the end of the war meant relief, gratitude, and the opportunity to return home.

---

80. Persico, 2004.
81. Persico, 2004.
82. Persico, 2004.
83. Library of Congress.

British soldier William Collins ended the war at an especially significant place: Mons. He recollected the fogginess of the Monday morning on November 11: "A silence came over the whole place that you could almost feel, you know, after four and a half years of war, not a shot was being fired, not a sound was heard because the fog blanketed everything, you see, and hug really thickly over. We were north-east of Mons…So there I was, back where the war started…"[84]

Clifford Lane reacted similarly: the fighting had worn him out, and he was glad just to be alive. In his unit, no one celebrated with alcohol; "we simply celebrated the armistice in silence and thankfulness that it was all over. And I believe that happened quite a lot in France."[85]

Ruby Ord, serving in France with the Women's Army Auxiliary Corps, also believed that those in France celebrated more quietly than those elsewhere just because of their proximity to the war: "I do think it was dampened down very much, in France. I think they had all the enthusiasm probably in England, but I think we were too near reality to feel that way. I didn't certainly."[86]

Others, like Charles Wilson of the Gloucestershire Regiment, were less pensive and focused more on celebrating the armistice: "[T]here was a swell of excitement amongst the men and our only interest then was to find something to drink to celebrate it and there was nothing to be had, not a bottle of wine or anything else! However we soon put that right…"[87]

Some like British Non-Commissioned Officer (NCO) Harry Forester took the merriment too far: "Now we'd arrived at Lille and the war was over and

---

84. "Podcast 47: Armistice."
85. "Podcast 47: Armistice."
86. "Podcast 47: Armistice."
87. "Podcast 47: Armistice."

all the sergeants were allowed out of barracks to go and have a drink. Of course we overdid it; everybody got drunk."[88]

By and large, the American response resembled the British and French response: some men were grateful, yet quiet while others were loud and joyful. Captain Harry Truman had arrived in France seven months earlier in April 1918 with 194 men in Battery D. When 11 a.m. on November 11 arrived, Truman was beyond grateful that all of his men had survived; not a single man from his battery died from April to November 1918.[89]

Colonel George C. Marshall, who would later become a prominent general in World War II, almost died a half hour before the war ended. Marshall, who graduated from Virginia Military Institute in 1902, originally planned and trained for the 1st Infantry Division and was then promoted in 1918 to work closely with General Pershing. An American pilot discharged a stuck bomb over the village of Souilly in northeastern France, which landed on a house that Marshall and others were using for headquarters. Although the explosion shook the house and threw Marshall against a wall and on the floor, Marshall survived the waning minutes of the war.[90]

> **Fun Fact**
>
> George Marshall was the architect of the Marshall Plan, which ran from 1948 to 1952 and gave money to recovering European countries after World War II. Many consider the plan a success at reviving the European economies and keeping Communism away from Western Europe. Three months after President Truman announced the Truman Doctrine to send aid to Greece and Turkey in June 1947, Secretary of State George Marshall proposed the Marshall Plan or the European Recovery Program – American financial aid for European recovery. President Truman

---

88. "Podcast 47: Armistice."
89. Persico, 2004.
90. Persico, 2004.

Chapter 6: Individual Responses to the Armistice   89

> assigned the first appropriation bill on April 3, 1948, authorizing $5.3 billion in aid to be sent to Europe. When the European Recovery Program ended on December 31, 1951, it had spent almost $12.5 billion in aid. The Marshall Plan is significant because, as some would argue, it contributed to the development of Europe after World War II as well as showcased the United States' charity; most countries did not send aid to other countries.

·ALL OUR COLOURS TO THE MAST·

Other Allied commanders feared that the Germans might use the armistice to regain their strength and begin fighting anew. General Pershing thought that the Allies should have defeated the Germans on the field to give them no opportunity to use the armistice to rearm. French General Charles Mangin also worried about the location of the signing. The armistice had been signed in the Forest of Compiègne, about 40 miles north of Paris.

Like Pershing and President of the French Republic, Raymond Poincaré, Mangin thought that it should have been signed in Berlin, meaning that the Allies would continue their offensives until they reached the German capital, because otherwise the Germans would not admit that they had been beaten. And, in fact, this very thing happened: some German textbooks do not ever mention the armistice.

Like Marshall, another important individual in World War II — Adolf Hitler — also recovered from an injury in the last hours of the war. In the late evening of October 13 and early morning of October 14, 1918, the British launched a mustard gas attack near Ypres, Belgium, which partially blinded Hitler and some of his friends. As Hitler recovered from the attack in Pasewalk military hospital in Prussia, he learned of the Kaiser's abdication and the armistice and resolved to enter politics and avenge Germany's downfall.

> **Did you know?**
>
> Adolf Hitler served on the front significantly longer than other soldiers from his regiment, the List Regiment. The Great War lasted slightly over fifty-one months, and Hitler served about forty-two of those months, meaning Hitler fought on the front for over eighty percent of World War I.[91]

Another big name of World War II, Hermann Göring, a leading Nazi Party member, Commander of the Luftwaffe, and the highest-ranking Nazi official tried at the Nuremberg War Crime Trials after World War II, also resented the armistice. Göring had served as an air ace (a military aviator

---

91. Weber, 2010.

credited with shooting down several enemy aircraft during aerial combat), flying with Baron Manfred von Richthofen "the Red Baron" in the "Flying Circus" during World War I. When Göring received a message that he had to turn over his squadron to the French near Strasbourg, he sent some aircraft to France and grounded the rest of the planes to junk near Darmstadt.[92]

Even some Allied troops felt terrible about all that the Germans had to surrender. George Fox of the Royal Navy who witnessed the surrender of Germany's High Seas Fleet remarked, "Well you know, that was the most pitiful sight that I think I shall ever see. To see such magnificent ships surrender to another fleet it was pitiful, really. You know, I could have cried, honestly I could…"[93]

As is expected, like Hitler and Göring, the German people did not celebrate the armistice. Instead, they viewed World War I as a defensive war in which they had proudly served their country and been punished for it. On November 12, 1918, Field Marshal Hindenburg wrote to the troops, "You kept the enemy away from our frontiers and you have saved your country from the misfortunes and disasters of war… Proud and with our head held high, we bring to an end the struggle in which we have held out for four years against a world filled with enemies."[94] The Germans could not understand why they had lost and why the Allies had treated them so harshly in the armistice. Some attributed their defeat in World War I to betrayal, for example the myth of the 'stab in the back.'[95] Others did not mention the end of the war at all. In some German school textbooks from the Weimar Republic (1919-1933), the German defeat was not mentioned: "chapters on the Great War ended with the final German offensives in the spring of

---

92. Persico, 2004.
93. "Podcast 47: Armistice."
94. Cited in Audoin-Rouzeau and Becker, 2002.
95. Audoin-Rouzeau and Becker, 2002.

1918."[96] Unlike the Allies who believed Germany and only Germany was to blame for the devastation that spread throughout Europe, Hindenburg viewed the war as a type of national crusade, portraying Germany as standing against the rest of the world. German commoners also shared a similar response. Historians Audoin-Rouzeau and Becker observe, "In many German towns, the soldiers were welcomed like conquerors by both the civilian populations and the authorities."[97]

But for those families who lost a relative, they began the mourning process. In one example, the portrait of a "dear departed brother" is placed between a Prussian and a Bavarian flag and pictures of Kaiser Wilhelm II and Prince Ruprecht of Bavaria. Directly above are a crucified Christ and an inscribed ribbon: "In memory of our beloved brother. The hero who died for the salvation of the Homeland!"[98]

---

96. Audoin-Rouzeau and Becker, 2002.
97. Audoin-Rouzeau and Becker, 2002.
98. Audoin-Rouzeau and Becker, 2002.

CHAPTER 7

Celebrations Around the World
11 a.m. on November 11, 1918

"You are Entitled to Rejoice"

Cities in the Allied countries erupted in celebration at 11 a.m. on November 11, 1918. Sir Edward Grey had famously said at the eruption of the war in 1914 that all the lamps in Europe had gone out and that he would not see them lit again in his lifetime. Although Grey was practically referring to the black outs necessary at night so that enemy fighters could not easily locate targets, he also spoke metaphorically that Europe was involved in such a devastating war that he did not expect to end quickly. Thankfully, he was wrong (he died in 1933). With the armistice signed, the lamps began to turn on all over Europe.

In London, England, Prime Minister Lloyd George exited his residence on 10 Downing Street and delivered a short oration at 11 a.m., telling the throngs of people who had crowded around him: "You are entitled to rejoice."[99] Later that afternoon in the House of Commons, the prime minis-

---

99. Persico, 2004.

ter read the terms of the armistice and concluded: "I hope we may say that thus, this fateful morning, came to an end all wars." Echoing H.G. Wells, Lloyd George shared the sentiments of many not only in Britain but also throughout the world.

> **Did you know?**
>
> 10 Downing Street is the Prime Minister's house in Great Britain. It is a recognizable address like 1600 Pennsylvania Avenue Northwest, the location of the White House.

The King and Queen of England, George V and Mary, entered the balcony of Buckingham Palace in the afternoon, showered by a small drizzle. Like the prime minister, King George V focused on the celebratory aspects of the armistice: "With you, I rejoice."

While the soldiers on the front found the quietness of the armistice stark and rejoiced by thanking God that they had survived, civilians celebrated much more boisterously. British officer William Chapman depicted the contrast of Armistice Day in the big cities and small towns versus in hospitals and on the battlefield: "[T]hat day particularly the mood that happened in London and other big towns was supposed to be exciting and thrilling…but in hospital amongst us wounded officers, there was perfect…I don't know, inhibition almost — perfect calm."[100] Church bells rang throughout the countryside, and crowds poured into the streets. In London, Big Ben rang for the first time since the beginning of the war in August 1914 in a 3 p.m. victory chime. People danced to choruses like Knees Up Mother Brown.

Mary Lees of the Air Ministry remembered the celebratory atmosphere of Armistice Day in London. Everyone was on the street in jubilant jamboree: "[Y]ou visualize every single office in Kingsway pouring down the Strand. I should think there must have been about 10,000 people. There was no traffic of course…Well, we didn't get back to the office, to our work, till about half past three, four…[N]obody would go inside because they all wanted to go on top and cheer."[101]

Future Prime Minister Winston Churchill depicted the stark contrast of the moments before and after 11 a.m. in London: "Then suddenly, the first stroke of the chime. I looked again at the broad street beneath me – it was deserted. Then, from all sides men and women came scurrying into the street…Almost before the last stroke of the clock had died away the strict, war-straitened, regulated streets of London had become a triumphant pandemonium. At any rate, it was clear that no more work would be done that day."[102]

---

100. "Podcast 47: Armistice."
101. "Podcast 47: Armistice."
102. "Podcast 47: Armistice."

Throughout the United Kingdom, people celebrated: some with Wurlitzer organs and patriotic songs and others in lorries (trucks) with little flags.[103] As Maisie Nightingale of Southampton recounted, "Yes, it was a wonderful day. I can remember that."[104]

For some, however, the end of the war brought happiness mingled with sadness. Vera Brittain, a nurse at the Queen Alexandra Hospital annex, had lost her brother, Edward, and her beau, Roland. She struggled with the celebrations — two men close to her had lost their lives so that others could celebrate. Vera could not get the two of them out of her mind. As she observed the lively celebrations around her, she reflected, "The War was over; a new age was beginning; but the dead were dead and would never return."[105]

---

103. "Podcast 47: Armistice."
104. "Podcast 47: Armistice."
105. Persico, 2004.

Basil Farrer, who had served on the Western Front, observed the crowds in Notthingham, but, like Vera Brittain, struggled to rejoice: "I remember Armistice Day and I didn't know at the time but in every city, everybody went mad. In London, they were dancing in the streets, the crowds, in all the cities, in Paris and in Nottingham too… I did not go there… I had a feeling of sadness. And I did remember all those chaps who'd never come back, because there was quit a lot, nearly a million…"[106]

The celebrations were more mixed in France, tending to be more somber, most likely because France had experienced more devastation. The French had been mixed in their opinions about giving the Germans an armistice instead of defeating them on the field. Many thought that the armistice was premature.[107] In the years after 1918, the French continued to differ on their opinions regarding the armistice; commemorations were torn "between happy celebrations of victory (and an end to the bloodshed) and sad

---

106. "Podcast 47: Armistice."
107. Douglas, 2002.

commemorations of the atrocious cost of the war."[108] A humorist for the French weekly The *Canard*, Rodolphe Bringer, faced the following dilemma in the 1926 armistice commemoration: if he should, "*to remain a good Frenchman*, weep or on the contrary party like a teenager."[109]

Across the Atlantic in the United States, the armistice celebrations were even more raucous, perhaps because America had not completely felt the effects of the war, separated by the thousands of miles across the ocean. Perhaps it was also due to the fact that Americans woke up to a Germany who had surrendered. For those living in the United States, World War I had ended at 6 a.m.

> **Fun Fact**
>
> The eastern most point of America — West Quoddy Head, Maine — was 5,500 miles away from one of the easternmost battlefields during World War I — Baghdad. Even the closest Western Front battlefield — Amiens — was over 3,000 miles away.

---

108. Douglas, 2002.
109. Douglas, 2002.

Parades and Kaiser effigy burnings appeared throughout America in small towns and big cities. In New York, Major John F. Hyland ordered the already scheduled bond-drive parade to go forward. Bands played songs like "Over There" and "Tipperary." A Kaiser Wilhelm effigy was burned in Central Park.

Massachusetts shoe laster (a person who attached the upper part of a shoe to the sole) James Hughes recounted the celebration in Boston: "There was a lot of excitement when we heard about the Armistice…some of them old fellas was walkin' on the streets with open Bibles [in] their hands. All the shops were shut down. I never seen the people so crazy…confetti was a-flying in all directions…I'll never forget it."[110]

Detroit also witnessed similar celebrations with confetti flying on Griswold Street, Lafayette Boulevard, and Michigan Avenue. A large crowd also gathered by the Soldiers' and Sailors' Monument in Campus Martius to celebrate the peace. The caption on one photo reads, "Monster Crowd Out."[111]

In Denver, Colorado, the euphoria resembled that of towns and cities across the United States and England. In fact, a Denver monthly newsletter published from 1909 to 1931, *Municipal Facts*, suggested that Armistice Day should become a holiday, which it eventually did in 1938. The November 1918 newsletter suggested that perhaps the new holiday could be called Liberty Day, Wilson Day, or Victory Day (anticipating V-E Day and V-J Day of World War II, Victory in Europe and Victory in Japan, respectively). Additionally, the newsletter suggested changing the date of Thanksgiving: "Another proposal is that Thanksgiving Day, instead of being celebrated on the last Thursday in November, should be fixed permanently on November 11."[112]

---

110. Library of Congress.
111. Gleit, 2015.
112. Rudolph, 2013.

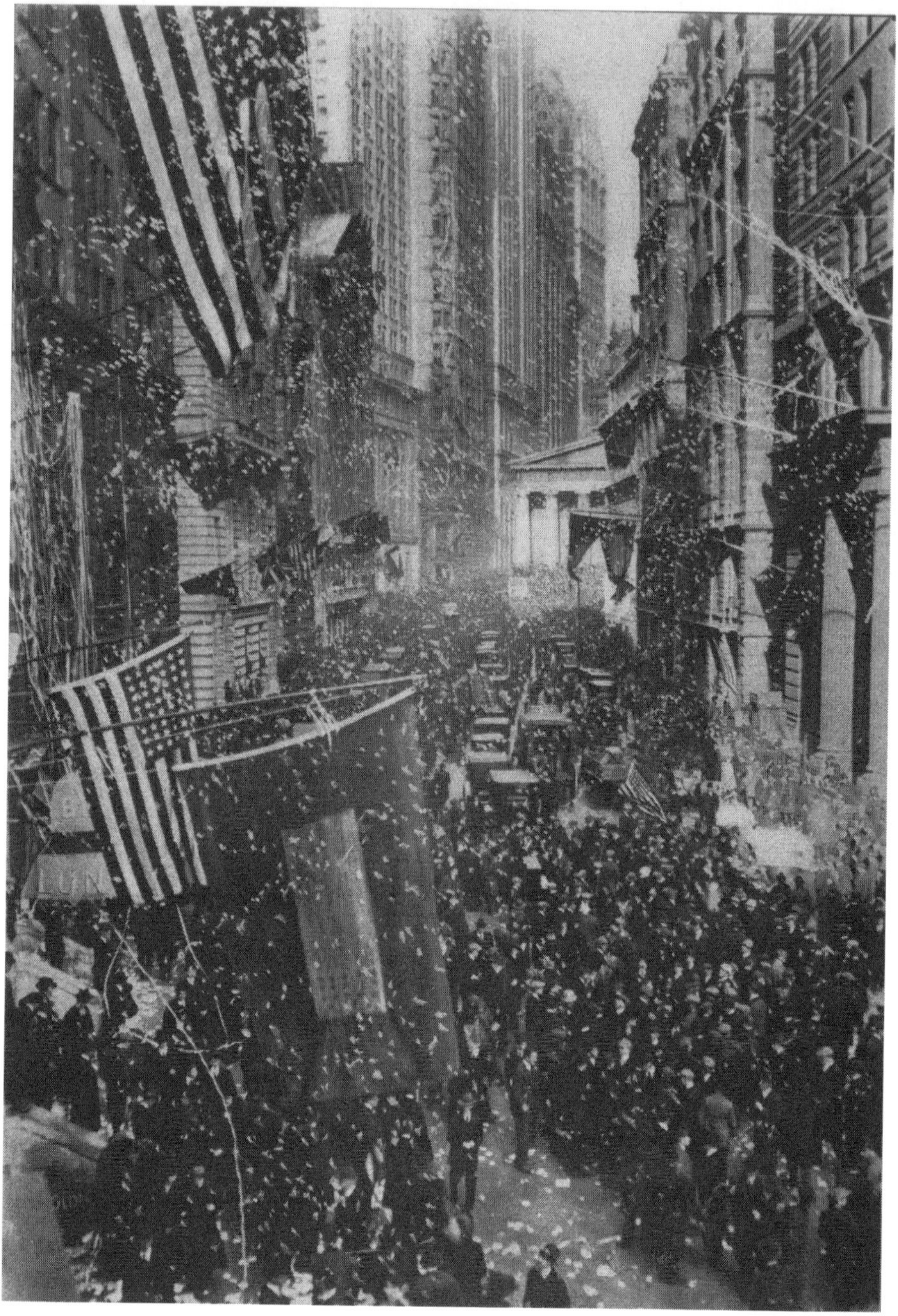

For some towns, the jubilation, parades, music, flags, firecrackers, and crowded streets of Armistice Day were unparalleled in the town's history. In Watertown, Wisconsin, the city went wild in a celebration that has never been surpassed, not even for the end of World War II.[113]

President Wilson issued a short Armistice Day proclamation, confident that America had made the right decision in joining World War I: "My fellow countrymen — The armistice was signed this morning. Everything for which America fought, has been accomplished. It will now be our fortunate duty to assist by example, by sober, friendly counsel, and by material aid, in the establishment of just democracy throughout the world. Woodrow Wilson."[114]

Slowly the news reached the extremities of the front. Bert Fearns, a Prisoner of War (POW) in Germany, learned of the armistice in a unique way. The Germans had a bulletin board to post information, and on November 11, there was simply one word: "Waffenstillstand." Fearns and his fellow POWs had learned a fair amount of German, but this was a new large word, so they asked for assistance from the sentry: "[H]e sort of looked up to heaven; put his rifle on the ground; and did a sort of Scots sword dance over it. So we knew by that, that the war was over."[115]

> **Did you know?**
>
> The German language is known for its long combination words. Waffenstillstand is an excellent example as it is the combination of three words: waffen (weapon), still (silent, calm, still), and stand (state, condition). In other words, waffenstillstand literally means the state of calm weapons, or a cease-fire. Thanks to Megan Korpics for parsing out the words!

---

113. Watertown *Daily Times*, 1952.
114. Philadelphia War History Committee, 1922.
115. "Podcast 47: Armistice."

Even though Malcolm Hancock and the West African Regiment learned of the armistice two days later on November 13 in Sierra Leone, they still commemorated the armistice: "I remember we lit an enormous bonfire; all the troops understood very well what the end of the war meant for them and they entered into the spirit of the thing very well…It was a terrific relief."[116]

President Wilson would proclaim the first Armistice Day a year later on November 11, 1919. While the original concept also included celebrating with a two-minute period of silence beginning at 11 a.m. and parades, Wilson focused more on the seriousness of the observance: "To us in America, the reflections of Armistice Day will be filled with solemn pride in the heroism of those who died in the country's service and with gratitude for

---

116. "Podcast 47: Armistice."

the victory, both because of the thing from which it has freed us and because of the opportunity it has given America to show her sympathy with peace and justice in the councils of the nations..."[117]

> **Fun Fact**
>
> During the 1920s, many cities in the United Kingdom hosted jubilant Armistice Balls to celebrate the end of the war. By the 1930s, however, the Armistice Day observances became more solemn and quiet. Armistice Balls have come back as today — one can dress up in 1920s attire and attend an Armistice Ball.

Lieutenant Robert Graves, who served in the First World War in the Royal Welch Fusiliers, depicted well the conflicting emotions on November 11, 1918 with his poem, "Armistice Day, 1918." The final two stanzas illustrate the contrast between the celebrating citizens and the deceased soldiers:

> "When the days of rejoicing are over,
> When the flags are stowed safely away,
> They will dream of another wild 'War to End Wars'
> And another wild Armistice day.
>
> But the boys who were killed in the trenches,
> Who fought with no rage and no rant,
> We left them stretched out on their pallets of mud
> Low down with the worm and the ant."

---

117. Library of Congress.

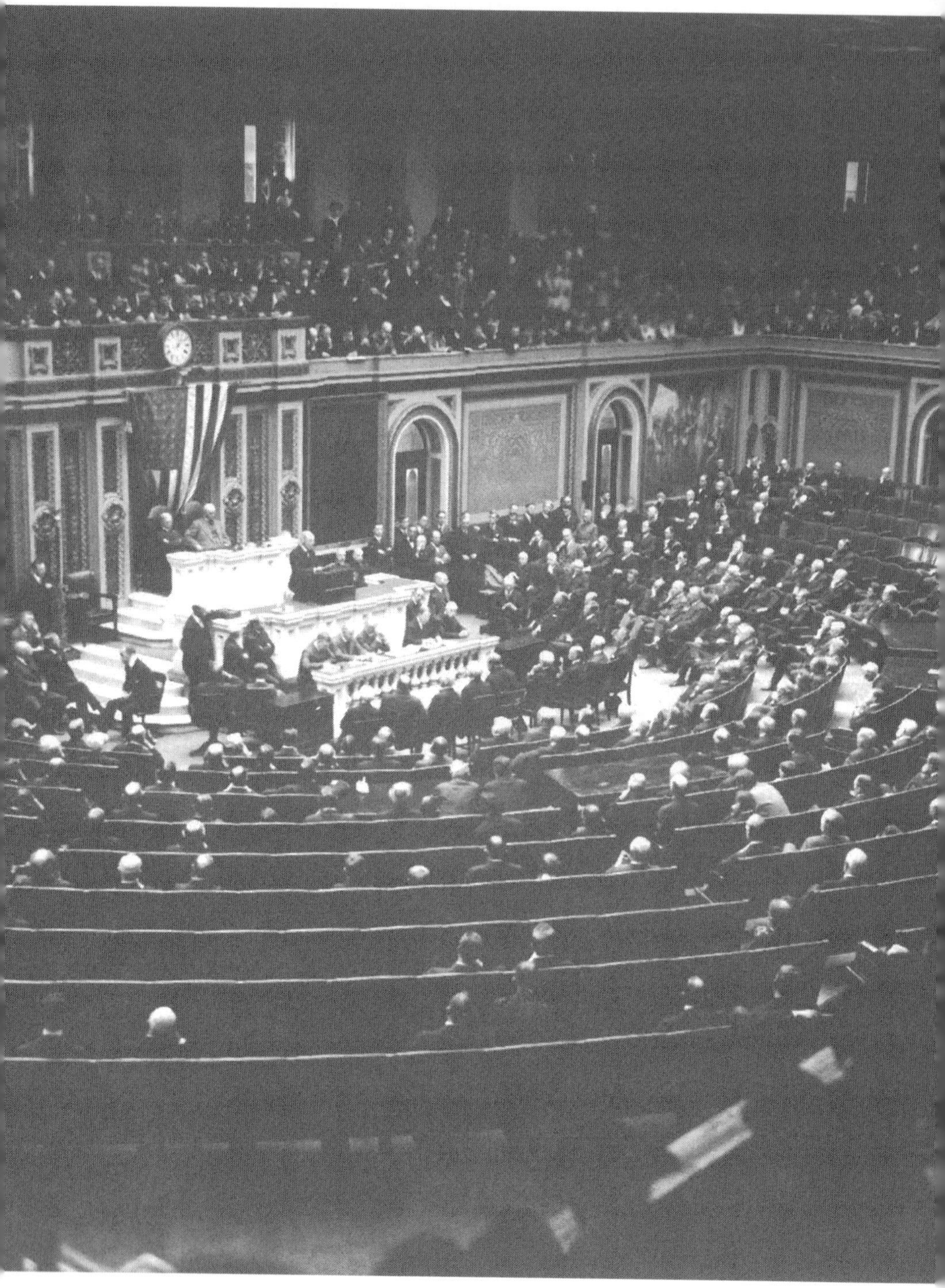

CHAPTER 8

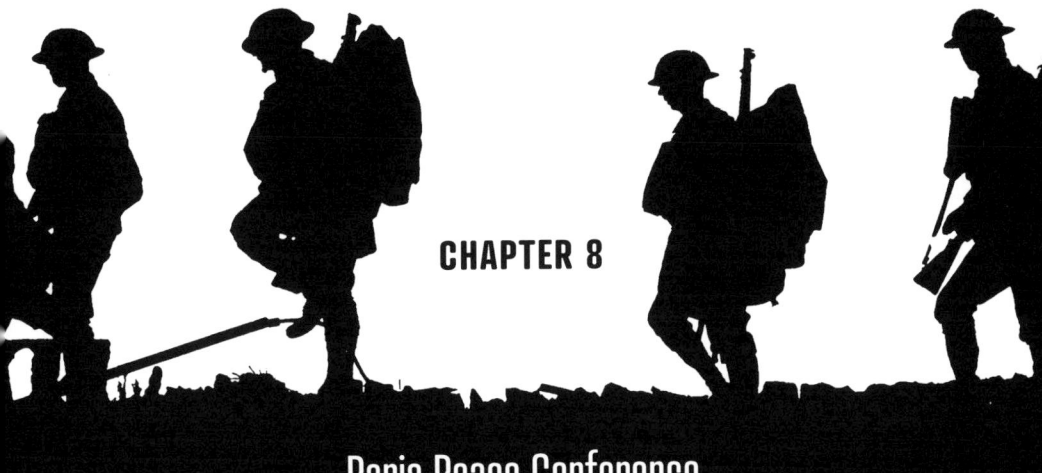

Paris Peace Conference
January 18, 1919–January 16, 1920

"The Brutal Peace"

The Paris Peace Conference began on January 18, 1919 when delegates from thirty-two nations convened to discuss the peace terms for Germany and its allies. The conference took place in Versailles, just outside Paris. As American diplomat Samuel Miller Breckinridge Long noted in his diary, "Today may be epoch marking in the history of the World. The Peace Conference opened its sessions in Paris with the representatives of the civilized world assembled around the board."[118] Because the Allied governments did not recognize the Bolshevik government, Russia was not invited to the peace conference; neither were the defeated Central Powers: Germany, Austria-Hungary, Turkey, and Bulgaria.[119] While Germany did attend the proceedings, they were not allowed to take part. Even though twenty-seven nations participated, the "Big Three" — the United Kingdom, France, and the United States — led the discussion. Originally, the

---

118. Long, 1919.
119. Office of the Historian.

Great Powers — the United Kingdom, France, the United States, Italy, and Japan — created the Council of Ten, which included the heads of state of their foreign ministers. Italy and Japan, however, showed little interest in anything except topics of local interest, so Wilson, Lloyd George, and Clemenceau made the major decisions. In the end, the conference oversaw the creation and signing of five different treaties with the Central Powers and the brief establishment of the League of Nations.

Fun Fact

President Woodrow Wilson was the first American president to visit Europe while in office. He arrived in December 1918 and made a stop in Reims, one of the largest cities in the Champagne region of France, two weeks after the Paris Peace Conference began.

The "Big Three" Representatives	
France	**Prime Minister Georges Clemenceau**
Great Britain	**Prime Minister David Lloyd George**
United States of America	**President Woodrow Wilson**

Fun Fact

One of my former students, Jack, believes that it is unfortunate that Bulgaria is often forgotten as a Central Power. At the onset of World War I, Bulgaria declared neutrality, but both sides (the Allied and Central powers) tried to entice Bulgaria to enter the war in their favor. Because the Central Powers had fewer smaller allies, they could offer Bulgaria more than the Triple Entente. Thus, Bulgaria committed to the Central Powers when the German military had the upper hand after the summer of 1915 and declared war on Serbia on October 1, 1915. Jack would frequently remind me that Bulgaria and Greece both touch Turkey, so this fun fact is written in honor of him and all my former students whose questions and curiosity inspire me to continue to learn.

Even though the "Big Three" fought together during World War I, they all disagreed with others about postwar settlements. The United States complicated the matter because it was an Associate Power that fought alongside the Allied Powers of France, Italy, and the United Kingdom and, as such, did not have to honor pre-existing agreements that focused on redistribution of territory among the other three parties.[120] Although President Woodrow Wilson opposed many arrangements, the treaties nonetheless shifted borders significantly. Alsace-Lorraine, acquired by the Germans after the Franco-Prussian War of 1870-1871, was returned to France, the Ottoman Empire disintegrated, Austria-Hungary was turned into two separate countries, and the Balkans, Africa, and Asia all saw substantial territorial changes.

---

120. Office of the Historian.

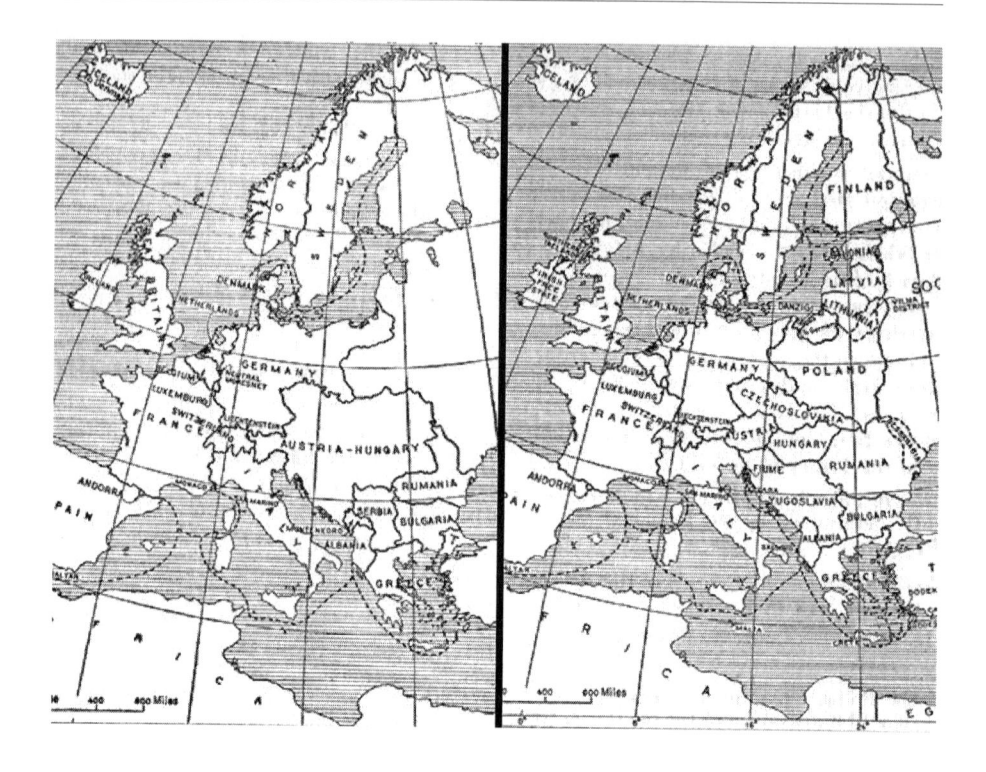

President Wilson and French Prime Minister Georges Clemenceau, nicknamed "Father Victory" or "The Tiger," differed greatly about how to handle Germany. Given that Germany had humiliated France during the Franco-Prussian War, Clemenceau and other French politicians took a tough stand against the Germans, wanting significant reparations and even suggesting substantial territorial gifts to France and Poland to ensure the Germany could never again attack France. Clemenceau was especially concerned about the Rhineland in western Germany and suggested making the Rhineland its own country. In one century, German armies had invaded France from the Rhineland four separate times (1814, 1815, 1870, and 1914). French Marshal Fayolle distrusted Wilson's League of Nations and believed that France needed a stronger assurance: "One speaks of the League, but what can this hypothetical society do without a means of action? One promises alliances, but alliances are fragile, like all human beings. There will always come a time when Germany will have a free hand.

Take all the alliances you want, but the greatest need for France and Belgium is a material barrier."[121]

Wilson, on the other hand, was much more interested in establishing a world of peace through the League of Nations and the principle of self-determination. Even after two months of discussion, two members of the "Big Four" could not agree. British Prime Minister Lloyd George remedied the situation by issuing the Fontainebleau Memorandum, which offered support for the League of Nations, on March 25 and then going with Wilson to Clemenceau on March 27 to offer France an alliance to ensure French security in the event of an attack. In addition, the War Guilt Committee had stated formally on March 29 that Germany was guilty of starting the war. Clemenceau gave up much of the French and Polish land claims, and, in turn, Wilson accepted a "war guilt" clause on April 5, convinced that the League of Nations would mitigate any difficulties in the peace terms. All agreed that a Reparations Commission would determine by May 1, 1921 the amount of and payment plan for the German reparations, which will be discussed more in-depth below.

> **Did you know?**
>
> Although Woodrow Wilson believed in self-determination and had assisted the Germans in seeking an armistice, he became increasingly frustrated with the German delegation at the Paris Peace Conference. When Count von Brockdorff-Rantzau tersely replied to the Allied offering of peace while seated, which was extremely rude, Wilson was incensed: "What abominable manners...The Germans are really a stupid people. They always do the wrong thing."[122] Others, like British Foreign Secretary Arthur Balfour, did not mind.

---

121. Dougall, 2017.
122. Johnson, 2010.

On May 7, 1919, five months after the conference had begun, the Allied powers gave the small German delegation the text of the treaty. Outraged, Germans considered the Treaty of Versailles "the brutal peace," and there was a mass demonstration in front of the Reichstag against the Treaty of Versailles about a week after the draft treaty came out on May 7. Even so, the treaty was fairly forbearing in contrast to the tough terms Germany gave Russia at Brest-Litovsk. Plus, the Versailles Treaty kept Germany mostly intact. After all, Germany retained 90 percent of its territory.

Of the 440 articles in the Treaty of Versailles, the first 26 laid out the covenant of the League of Nations while the final 414 dealt with Germany's punishment. The Treaty of Versailles can be summarized into three sections: the League of Nations, border adjustment and military depletion, and German reparations and war guilt.

The concept for the League of Nations came from President Wilson's "Fourteen Points" address to the United States Congress on January 8, 1918. Beginning in 1917, the year in which America entered World War I, Wilson had delivered several speeches that discussed his vision for ending the war in a way that would bring a "just and secure peace," rather than "a new balance of power." Wilson delineated a specific program in his "Fourteen Points" speech. Of the fourteen points, eight dealt with specific territorial concerns, five pertained to general principles for a peaceful world, and the last point encouraged the development of what would become the League of Nations. As Wilson stated, the only possible program for the world's peace included this: "A general association of nations must be formed under specific covenants for the purpose of affording mutual guarantees of political independence and territorial integrity to great and small states alike."[123]

> **Fun Fact**
> President Wilson received a Nobel Peace Prize in October 1919 for his efforts to establish and promote the League of Nations.

When Wilson first proposed his ideas, they were extremely popular to the European nations — all were exhausted from four years of war. Wilson was able to use his influence to ensure that the Covenant of the League of Nations was included in Part I of the Treaty of Versailles. The covenant delineated the main organs and the chief goals of the League of Nations. The League would have an Assembly of all members, a Council made up of five permanent members and four rotating members, and an International Court of Justice. The official languages were French, English, and Spanish. As for the aims of the League, it intended to guarantee collective security, disarmament, and open diplomacy, provided means for arbitration and judicial settlement, and purported to encourage international cooperation in economic and social issues.

---

123. Wilson, 1918.

While the League experienced some criticisms, especially given that Wilson no longer represented the views of mainstream America, it was generally well received. Additionally, even though the United States did not join the League, the first meeting was held immediately after the ratification of the Versailles Treaty.

ORIGIN OF THE LEAGUE OF NATIONS

January 8th, 1918. Fourteen Points laid down by President Wilson as the basis of world peace. (*)

January 25th, 1919. League accepted in principle.

April 28th, 1919. Covenant adopted.

January 10th, 1920. League came into being; Secretariat established in London.

January 16th, 1920. First meeting of Council at Paris.

November 1st, 1920. League Headquarters moved from London to Geneva.

November 15th, 1920. First Meeting of Assembly at Geneva.

Woodrow WILSON

(*) THE FOURTEENTH POINT:
"A General Association of Nations must be formed under specific covenants for the purpose of affording mutual guarantees of political independence and territorial integrity to great and small States alike."

> **Did you know?**
>
> When Wilson referenced "balance of power," he was referring to the result of the Napoleonic Wars. The four European powers that had defeated Napoleon — Russia, Prussia, Britain, and Austria — convened the Congress of Vienna from 1814 to 1815 to establish a new balance of power that would prevent French imperialism (as demonstrated by Napoleon) and would maintain peace between the powers. As a result, Prussia gained some westward territory to reduce the strength of France. The four European powers (and later France, which joined as a fifth power at the conference) wanted to ensure that no state would become strong enough to threaten the other powers.

Germany was forbidden to join the League of Nations and lost ten percent of its land due to the Treaty of Versailles. Great Britain and France received all of Germany's colonies while a variety of countries acquired land from Germany. France finally regained the Alsace-Lorraine region, which it had lost in 1871 to the Germans. The Belgians received the regions of Eupen and Malmedy in western Germany while North Schleswig was given to Denmark. Poland obtained the rich farmland of Posen in eastern Germany. The Rhineland in Western Germany near France and Belgium was demilitarized, meaning that Germany could not place any troops in the area next to France. Germany was also forbidden from *Anschluss* (union) with Austria to its south so that the former could not regain its erstwhile strength. Finally, Danzig — now Gdańsk, Poland — on the Baltic Sea became a free city run by the League of Nations.

In additional to significant territorial losses, Germany's military was greatly reduced. The treaty forbade Germany from having an air force or submarines. While Germany could have an army and navy, it was considerably smaller: the army could have no more than 100,000 men and the navy could only have six battleships.

Articles 231 and 232 required that Germany, as the guilty party, make reparations, or the paying of debts to those who have been wronged, to the Allied countries. The former established Germany's guilt for the war while the latter listed the reparations. In addition to this civil law obligation, some of the Allied countries, namely Britain and the United States, insisted that Germany was also morally responsible for the war: "[While the French Prime Minister Georges Clemenceau] believed that the Germans should be denied any opportunity of revenge, the Anglo-Saxons (Wilson and Prime Minister Lloyd George) believed anything perceived as injustice would only lead to a recurrence of war."[124] The treaty also allowed for the trial of

---

124. Audoin-Rouzeau and Becker, 2002.

Kaiser Wilhelm II and other high-ranking German officials as war criminals.

> **Fun Fact**
>
> After World War II, the United States, Britain, and France oversaw the development of one side of Germany (Western Germany) while the Soviet Union paid attention to the other side (Eastern Germany). This split took place because the first three governments believed in democratic republicanism while the Soviet Union believed in communism, and splitting Germany into two parts was a way to bring peace among the Allies.

An international reparations committee took two years to assess the German economy and to decide how much the Germans could afford in reparations. Originally, the Germans were required to repay 266 gold marks, or roughly $63 billion then or $768 billion at today's rate, but that was later reduced to $33 billion then or $402 billion today.[125] In order to make its first payment of $500 million in August 1921, the German government just printed paper money, which it continued to do, leading to the hyperinflation of 1923 (more on this topic in Chapter 10). Throughout the 1920s, the Germans defaulted several times on their reparations, and, by 1933, Hitler had cancelled all reparations. In 1953 at an international meeting later known as the London Agreement, Western Germany agreed to slowly pay back the defaulted bonds of the 1920s.[126] Western Germany gave only one stipulation: it would not finish repaying the bonds until Germany was reunited. In 1990, Germany reunified, now known as German Unity Day and celebrated on October 3, and, in 1995, Germany began to settle all its debts.[127] Of course, the interest has been adjusted downward several times; otherwise the interest on the unpaid bonds would

---

125. Suddath, 2010.
126. Suddath, 2010.
127. Suddath, 2010.

be astronomical. On October 3, 2010, 92 years after World War I ended, the Germans finished paying the reparations debt, thus settling its World War I accounts.[128]

> **Did you know?**
>
> British economist John Maynard Keynes strongly disagreed with the Allied decision to give Germany such high reparations. In fact, he quit the Paris Peace Conference in protest and returned to Britain to write *The Economic Consequences of Peace* in which he posited the reparations would devastate the German economy.[129] He also included a cutting critique of Wilson and argued that the economic clauses would harm European recovery overall. Although modern historians now believe that the fines were realistic, albeit large, many economists in the 1920s agreed with Keynes.

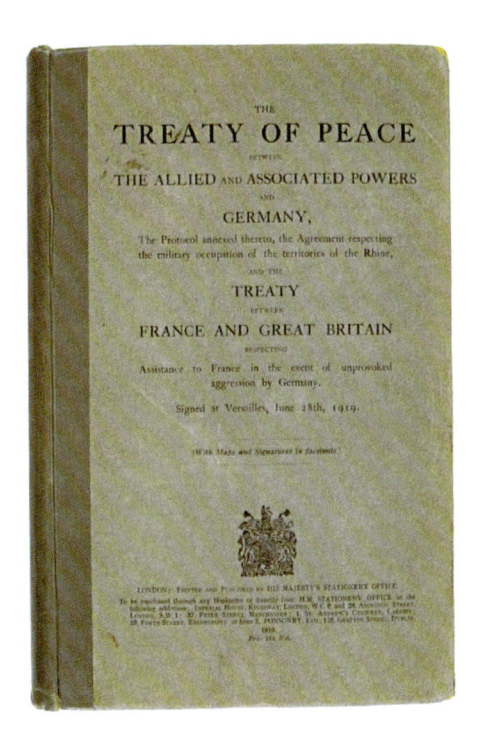

---

128. Suddath, 2010.
129. Suddath, 2010.

On June 16, Germany received the final treaty, and two weeks later, the Allies and the Germans signed the Treaty of Versailles. Crowds surged around Versailles Palace after the treaty was officially signed on June 28, 1919. The Weimar government, which consisted of Democrats, Social Democrats, and the Catholic Center party, ratified the treaty on July 9, 1919.

Certainly one of the more unpopular treaties created, the Treaty of Versailles was disliked all around. The Germans obviously did not appreciate the fairly stringent terms, especially articles 231 and 232. Several Britons disagreed with the Wilsonian idealism of the treaty. Perhaps, however, the most condemning disapproval came from the American government. Various political groups in the United States (nationalists, xenophobes, protectionists, and isolationists) all condemned Wilsonianism and the League of Nations. The nation whose president had suggested the League of Nations did not even ratify the treaty or join the League, thus greatly decreasing the prestige, appeal, and success of the League of Nations. Although the League of Nations officially lasted for twenty-six years from 1920 to 1946 when the United Nations replaced it and took over its duties, its power waned in the 1930s and was practically non-existent by 1939.

> **Fun Fact**
>
> The United States actually signed a separate treaty with Germany because the Treaty of Versailles fell short of ratification by seven votes due to its inclusion of the League of Nations. The Treaty of Berlin, signed on August 25, 1921, allowed the United States to receive all "rights, privileges, indemnities, reparations or advantages," but did not mention the League of Nations.[130]

---

130. Office of the Historian.

The delegates continued to work on additional treaties after presenting the Treaty of Versailles to the Germans. The Treaty of Saint-Germain ended the war with the Austrians and was signed on September 10. The Treaty of Neuilly, which brought peace with Bulgaria, was signed on November 27. Although the Paris Peace Conference was officially concluded with the formal inauguration of the League of Nations on January 16, 1920, treaties with Turkey and Hungary were not concluded until 1920 (with a later revision to the former in 1923).

Although Adolf Hitler certainly embodied the breaking of the Treaty of Versailles, the Germans had been breaking it well before 1933 when Hitler came to power. They purchased weapons from the Soviet Union, which ignored the provision in the Treaty of Versailles that stated the Germans could not amass a large army.[131] In Laura Hillenbrand's national bestseller *Unbroken*, World War II veteran Louie Zamperini recounted a particularly

---

131. Johnson, 2009.

prominent and blatant display of German military power despite the restrictions in the Treaty of Versailles. When other nations arrived in Berlin for the 1936 Olympics, the Nazis put on a great display of strength: "Military units drilled openly, and though powered aircraft were forbidden under the Versailles Treaty, the strength of the burgeoning Luftwaffe was on conspicuous display over an airfield, where gliders swooped over impressed tourists and Hitler."[132]

---

132. Hillenbrand, 2010.

CHAPTER 9

Military Leaders and Politicians After World War I

"Chained to the Germany of 1918"

Douglas MacArthur

Remember Douglas MacArthur, the general who was temporarily captured as a German spy when General Liggett ignored the traditional boundaries between the units in the rush to retake Sedan? General MacArthur became an extremely prominent figure in World War II and the years after. After World War I, MacArthur served as Superintendent of the United States Military Academy at West Point from 1919 to 1922. In 1925, he became the army's youngest major general. When MacArthur retired from the army in 1937, he served as Military Advisor to the Filipino government. In 1941, MacArthur was recalled to duty to serve as Commander of the Allies Forces in the Southwest Pacific during World War II. Many soldiers like the author's grandfather who fought in the Philippines greatly respected MacArthur, and the general was extremely popular among the men. MacArthur accepted Japan's surrender on September 2, 1945 and oversaw the occupation of Japan from 1945 to 1951. When the Korean War began in 1950, MacArthur served as Commander-in-Chief of the United Nations Command (UNCOM) and was later fired by President Truman on March 10, 1951 for differences in military strategy of the Korean War and for making public statements on policy matters. The American people, who had always liked MacArthur, were extremely upset that Truman had removed a beloved general and Truman's approval ratings dropped substantially to 22 percent (even though he had started his term at an 87 percent approval rating).

Did you know?

Even Lyndon Johnson, Richard Nixon, and George Bush all had higher Gallup approval ratings than Truman at the most unpopular times of their presidencies (the Vietnam War, Watergate, and the Iraq War respectively).[133]

---

133. Gallup, 2017.

Harry Truman

As briefly stated above, Captain Harry Truman of Battery D — who did not lose any of his 194 men in seven months — would become one of the most prominent figures near the end of World War II and during the years immediately following the Second World War. Truman became a Senator in 1934 and headed the Senate Special Committee to Investigate the National Defense Program during World War II, examining potential waste and corruption. When wartime President Franklin D. Roosevelt died on April 12, 1945, FDR's vice-president Truman became America's 33rd president. He made the decision, which is still debated by historians and citizens alike, to drop two atomic bombs on Hiroshima and Nagasaki on August 6 and 9, 1945 respectively, which ended the war with Japan, and stood by that decision his entire life.

Truman would be known for his foreign policy during his administration. In March 1947, Truman asked Congress for $400 million in aid to Greece and Turkey to save them from Communism. In 1948, Truman oversaw the massive airlift to Western Berlin when the Russians blockaded those sectors, and, in 1949, he helped establish the North Atlantic Treaty Organization (NATO).

Modeled after FDR's New Deal, Truman's domestic program, the Fair Deal, was introduced in January 1949 because he believed "every segment of our population and every individual has a right to expect from our government a fair deal." It was a mixed success because he had several lost cause laws (civil rights legislation, Taft-Hartley repeal, aid to education, Brannan plan, and national health insurance), and he really only achieved one goal: the Housing Act of 1949. The Fair Deal was significant because it showed

Truman's commitment to FDR's initiatives and Truman's weakness as a president because he seemed to focus more on his foreign policy.

When the communist government of North Korea invaded South Korea on June 25, 1950 (later seen as the "Pearl Harbor" of the Korean War, due to the surprise), President Truman did not ask Congress for a declaration of war, but instead ordered U.S. air and sea forces to assist South Korea on June 27, 1950. Korea was significant because it forced Truman to put his domestic policies on the back burner and quite possibly was the reason why he didn't run a third time. In fact, Truman's failure in handling the Korean War, the first large armed conflict of the Cold War, led to the election of big name general Dwight Eisenhower "Ike" in November 1952.

George Patton

George Patton, who was one of the most controversial and indiscreet generals during World War II, also played a significant role in World War I. Before the start of the Great War, Patton had served as the aide to General

Pershing, who later became Commander of the United States Troops in World War I. In May 1917, Patton joined Pershing and others to ship out to Europe. Along with Dwight D. Eisenhower, Captain Patton was supposed to start an American Expeditionary Force (AEF) Light Tank School. After receiving training in France, Patton then was briefed on the result of the largest-to-date tank battle of World War I from Colonel Fuller, the chief of staff for the British Tank Corp. Patton received the first ten tanks of the Haute-Marne-Tank School in March 1917, most of which he had to drive because no one else knew how to drive them.[134] Now Major Patton was in charge of training tank crews to assist the infantry. When Patton was promoted to Lieutenant Colonel and put in charge of the U.S. 1st Provisional Tank Brigade several months later, he was responsible to oversee the logistics of U.S. tanks in World War I, the first U.S. use of tanks in combat. Although Patton, now colonel in the Tanks Corps of the U.S. National Army, was on the field on November 11, he did not experience any further action because he had been wounded earlier and had only just returned to duty on October 28.[135]

> **Fun Fact**
>
> George Patton and Dwight Eisenhower worked together on the development of tanks with Patton serving in France and Eisenhower in Camp Meade, Maryland. Both argued against conventional tactical procedure and were in favor of utilizing tanks "as a separate arm of the fighting force."[136] After World War I when the funding toward tank development was nearly depleted, both Patton and Eisenhower were reassigned. In fact, only one tank prototype was built between 1925 and

---

134. Armed Forces Museum, 2013.
135. Armed Forces Museum, 2013.
136. Williams and Shaffer, 2015.

> **1931.**[137] When Douglas MacArthur became Chief of Staff of the Army, he sponsored some experimentation efforts to bring back tanks in offensives.[138] Thanks to Lieutenant Colonel Gil Petrina (ret.) for passing along this article!

After World War I, Patton continued to assist with tank development — although he is best known for his swift conquest of Sicily, his rapid push through France in World War II, and his unfortunate decision to slap two soldiers suffering from shell shock. The Nazis respected Patton's military prowess and considered him the best general the United States had. Patton's rash act in slapping two soldiers and the German's deep admiration for him as a general made him the perfect candidate to command a ghost army to distract the Germans and keep them from finding out about Operation Overlord, or D-Day. Operation Quicksilver, as Patton's ghost army was called, did successfully fool the Germans and saved countless lives on June 6, 1944. Unlike MacArthur, Patton remained a notorious figure, greatly honored by the Germans, but less recognized by their American peers.

> **Did you know?**
>
> Patton competed in the 1912 Olympics in Stockholm, Sweden in the first pentathlon against forty-two other people. He finished overall in fifth place.[139]

---

137. Williams and Shaffer, 2015.
138. Williams and Shaffer, 2015.
139. Armed Forces Museum, 2013.

Winston Churchill

Perhaps the most iconic figure of World War II, Winston Churchill, continued to rise in prominence after World War I. Former First Lord of the Admiralty Churchill became Prime Minister in England on May 10, 1940 when Neville Chamberlain's appeasement of Hitler became so unpopular that Chamberlain had to step down. Churchill used the lessons he had learned from World War I (the failure of the Dardanelles campaign and his time on the field) as Prime Minister during World War II. He rallied the British people (as well as served as an inspiration for many Americans) and saved Britain from the brink of defeat with his beautiful orations, clear-sighted leadership, and quick wit. From the successful evacuation of over 300,000 Allied troops at Dunkirk from May 26 to June 4, 1940 to fostering a friendship with American president Franklin D. Roosevelt in order to stand as an Anglo-American against the Nazis to refusing to give into Adolf Hitler, Churchill defined British politics during World War II. When the Liberal party regained control in 1945, Churchill left the office of Prime Minister only to return again in 1951 until 1955. He was known for his refusal to accept Communism and his concerns about Josef Stalin and Soviet Russia.

In addition to his political prowess, Churchill was also a renowned amateur historian, and his notable works include *A History of the English-Speaking Peoples, 1956-1958* and *The Second World War, 1948-1953*. His prose style is unequaled; you would probably recognize a lot of Churchill's phrases, but you may not realize that he wrote them. For example, on May 13, 1940, Churchill warned the House of Commons of the challenges that Britain faced in opposing Hitler: "I have nothing to offer but blood, toil, tears and sweat." Another famous example is his ubiquitous (appearing everywhere!) use of the word "fight" in a speech delivered after the Allied troops at Dunkirk had been successfully rescued:

> "We shall go on to the end, we shall fight in France, we shall fight on the seas and oceans, we shall fight with growing confidence and growing strength in the air, we shall defend our Island, whatever the cost may be, we shall fight on the beaches, we shall fight on the landing grounds, we shall fight in the fields and in the streets, we shall fight in the hills; we shall never surrender, and even if, which I do not for a moment believe, this Island or a large part of it were subjugated and starving, then our Empire beyond the seas, armed and guarded by the British Fleet, would carry on the struggle, until, in God's good time, the New World, with all its power and might, steps forth to the rescue and the liberation of the old."

> **Fun Fact**
>
> Winston Churchill popularized the phrase "iron curtain" frequently used during the Cold War (1946-1991) in his "Sinews of Peace" speech on March 5, 1946, delivered at Westminster College in Fulton, Missouri.

While all of these men played a less prominent role in World War I, they became big names during World War II. For others, like Henri Pétain, they had more influence during World War I and sometimes more, sometimes less power during World War II.

Henri Pétain

Pétain, the general who stopped the Germans at Verdun and who was sometimes known as the Lion of Verdun, became the French premier (Prime Minister) after Germany invaded France in 1940 and surrendered half of France to the Nazis. From July 1940 to August 1944, he served as chief of state for the rump Vichy government. Since Pétain turned 84-years-old in 1940, he ranks as France's oldest head of state. After World War II, Chairman of the Provisional Government of the Republic and later President of France Charles de Gaulle sentenced Pétain for treason. Although Pétain originally faced a death sentence, de Gaulle commuted the sentence to life in prison given Pétain's age and his service during World War I. Pétain died in prison on July 23, 1951.

> **Did you know?**
>
> Like the Weimar Republic in Germany named for the town in which the government resided, Vichy France was also named for the spa town in which the government resided. Pétain and others in the government voted to change the French Third Republic into the French State, an authoritarian regime.

Count Helldorf

Count Helldorf, the young German who delivered the news of the armistice to the Kaiser, later became police chief in Berlin. He joined the Nazi party in 1925, but as the Second World War progressed, had increasing doubts about Adolf Hitler and joined the conspiracy to overthrow the Führer Helldorf was in Berlin to assist with Operation Valkyrie, Colonel von Stauffenberg's attempt to assassinate Hitler and stage a coup on July 20, 1944. Arrested by the Gestapo that same day, Helldorf was convicted of treason and hanged for his involvement in the conspiracy on August 15, 1944.

Kaiser Wilhelm II

Under the Treaty of Versailles, Kaiser Wilhelm II, who had abdicated just before the armistice was signed, faced charges as a war criminal. However, the Netherlands, where he had fled, did not give him up. He died in Doorn in 1941, which the Nazi government invaded and occupied in May 1940. The Netherlands was not liberated

Erich Ludendorff

Erich Ludendorff, at one point the German Army chief of staff, became an ultranationalist and marched with Hitler in 1923 in an unsuccessful attempt to seize Bavaria. He was elected to the Reichstag in 1924 as a representative of the Nazi party, but gradually had a falling out with Hitler. When Hitler became Chancellor in 1933, Ludendorff no longer supported him. In 1925, Ludendorff had run for president, losing in a second round to his former superior, Hindenburg, with whom Ludendorff had served during World War I. Humiliated, Ludendorff broke off his friendship with Hindenburg and died in 1937 before Hitler and the Nazis rose to the strength they had in the early years of World War II.

Friedrich Ebert

When Friedrich Ebert, the chancellor who had taken over for Prince Max and negotiated the armistice with the Allies, died in 1925, Hindenburg was elected Germany's second president. Reelected in 1932, the then senile president named Hitler chancellor in 1933. When Hindenburg died in 1934, Hitler seized power. Although Ludendorff had lost touch with the German people by the time he died, Hindenburg was still a revered national figure.

Adolf Hitler

More than any other politician or military leader, World War I transformed Adolf Hitler's life. As the armistice was signed, Hitler was in a hospital recovering from a gas attack. He promised himself that if he got well, he would get involved in politics. Hitler intended to reverse the actions of the so-called November criminals and to reestablish Germany as the most powerful country in Europe: "My programme from the first was to abolish the Treaty of Versailles . . . I have written it thousands of times. No human being has ever declared or recorded what he wanted more than me."[140]

In 1940, French writer and war veteran Georges Bernanos declared that the driving force of Hitler was his past experiences in World War I: "The master of Germany is really its slave: he is chained to the Germany of 1918, to his country's defeat and dishonor, so that even triumph would be wrapped in bitterness and equal to his hatreds…"[141] Although some people focus on Hitler and what he hoped to accomplish for Germany — creating a world empire and improving the economy — in many respects, Hitler was more focused on the past than the future. Hitler wanted to avenge Germany's honor. Had World War I never happened, there is a good chance that World War II would have never been fought either. And perhaps more starkly, had the Allies not insisted on such stringent armistice terms, there is a chance that Hitler's rise to power might have been less likely.

---

140. Johnson, 2009.
141. Cited in Audoin-Rouzeau and Becker, 2002.

> **Fun Fact**
>
> An easy way to remember why Hitler disliked the Treaty of Versailles is the acronym "BRAT." First, the treaty *Blamed* Germany for causing World War I, even assigning moral responsibility. Second, the treaty required Germany to *Repay* the Allied Powers. Third, the treaty obliterated the German *Army*. Finally, the treaty took away all of Germany's *Territories* and colonies.

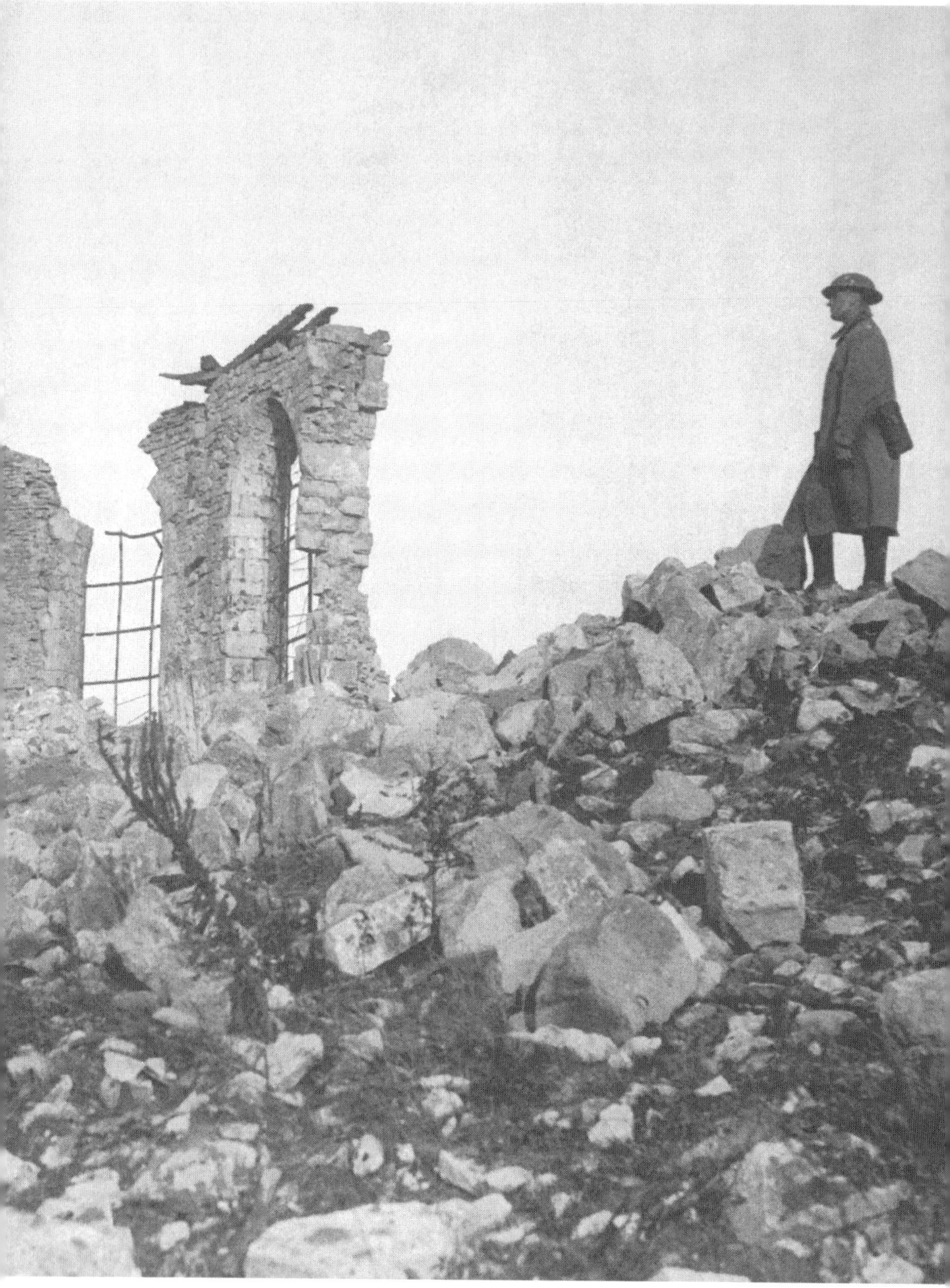

CHAPTER 10

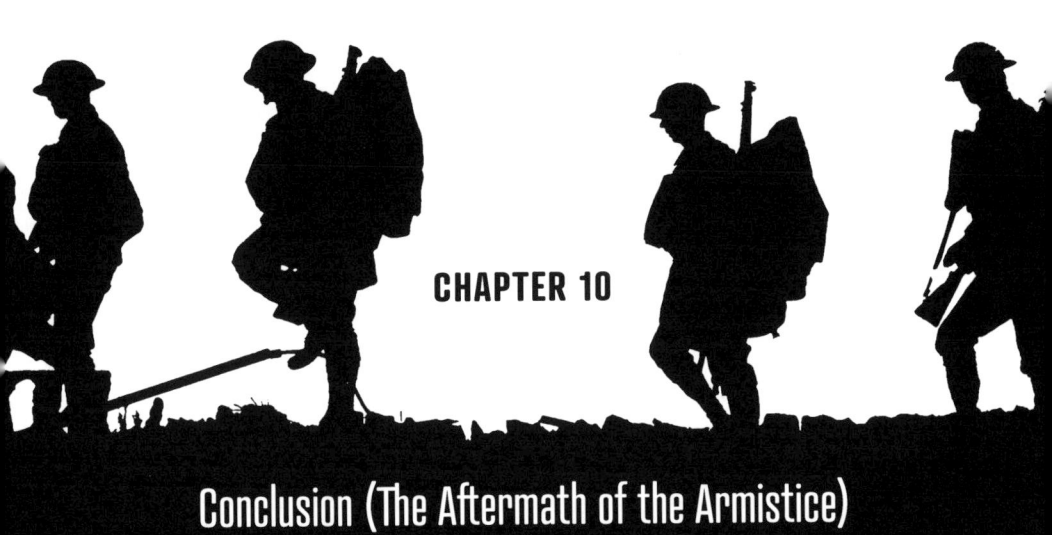

Conclusion (The Aftermath of the Armistice)

"The Recording of An Heroic Gesture"

With the signing of the Treaty of Versailles, World War I officially came to an end on June 28, 1919, exactly five years after the assassination of Archduke Ferdinand had precipitated the war. Roughly two weeks later on Bastille Day (July 14), France's national holiday, French and other Allied soldiers paraded down the Champs-Elysées in the Défilé de la Victoire, or the March of Victory.[142]

In some aspects, it could be said that World War I had achieved its practical war aim: liberate Belgium. But at what cost? The war was over, and there was peace, but all throughout Europe, one could see the devastation caused by the war. Towns, churches, and families were all destroyed. Famous French novelist and essayist Marcel Proust reflected on these ruins in 1918, remembering the splendor of the cathedrals north of Paris he had visited before the war: "I admire and weep more for the soldiers than for the

---

142. Kladstrup and Kladstrup, 2006.

churches, which were only the recording of an heroic gesture that today is reenacted at every moment."[143] In other words, Proust acknowledges that the demolition of beautiful buildings is depressing; yet every day, families who were bereaved have to suffer their loss daily. The churches and other buildings can be rebuilt; a lost son, brother, husband, or father will never return.

Ypres, Belgium illustrates well the damage wrought by World War I. The famous Cloth Hall, begun in the year 1200, was almost completely decimated. The cathedral nearby did not fare much better. Just as holidays would remind families of their bereavement, these gaping holes where buildings used to be reminded civilians of the totality of the war.

---

143. Cited in Audoin-Rouzeau and Becker, 2002.

Before   **After**

The wine regions in France, especially Champagne, were hit hard by the Great War. Interestingly, though the wine regions experienced great turmoil in 1914, the year that everyone expected their boys to be back by Christmas, many consider the 1914 to be the greatest champagne of the century. Maurice Pol-Roger, executive of Pol-Roger, a wine house known for its champagnes — they were Winston Churchill's favorite champagne — , and oenophiles, experts on wines, called the 1914 "the wine of victory."[144]

In addition to the immense devastation Europe, especially France, experienced, World War I had several repercussions directly connected to the events of the war. To begin with, the war caused a general inflationary period in Europe during the 1920s. This inflation hit Germany particularly hard due to the reparations, which led to the hyperinflation of the German Reichsmark by 1923. After the war, Germany had to pay pensions and reparations, and no country would loan it money. The German central bank decided to print significant amounts of money and loan said money to the government, resulting in perhaps the most damaging example of inflation in history.

---

144. Kladstrup and Kladstrup, 2006.

> **Fun Fact**
>
> Historian Carl Ludvig-Holtfrerich gives the famous example of someone sitting in a German pub in the 1920s and ordering a beer. When the waiter brings the customer the beer, he immediately orders another beer. The waiter pauses, "You haven't finished!" The customer replies, "True, but if I don't order now, the prices will double by the time I finish this first beer!"[145]

The mark-dollar exchange rate rose from 4.2 to 1 in 1914 to 4.2 trillion to 1 in 1923, less than ten years![146] Children would play with marks, and it became cheaper to burn marks than firewood. As *The Economist* notes, "[a]t its height, prices were rising so fast that waiters had to climb on tables to call out new menu prices in restaurants every half hour. Banknotes became sufficiently useless that workers had to bring wheelbarrows with them to work to collect their daily pay…"[147] The mark was used as wallpaper in bathrooms, and it even cost one million marks to mail a letter at the mark's highest inflation![148] Some connect the rise of Nazism to hyperinflation, but academics like British historian Frederick Taylor suggest that the deflation in the 1930s was more instrumental in bringing Hitler and the Nazis to power. After all, "The Nazi party did not become a popular political force until long after the hyperinflation period ended. The Nazis only won 32 Reichstag seats in the election of May 1924, and just 12 in 1928."[149]

---

145. Kenney and Chace, 2011.
146. *The Economist*, 2013.
147. *The Economist*, 2013.
148. Kenney and Chace, 2011.
149. *The Economist*, 2013.

Chapter 10: Conclusion (The Aftermath of the Armistice) 137

1 "Gold"Mark = "Reichs"Mark 1918-1924

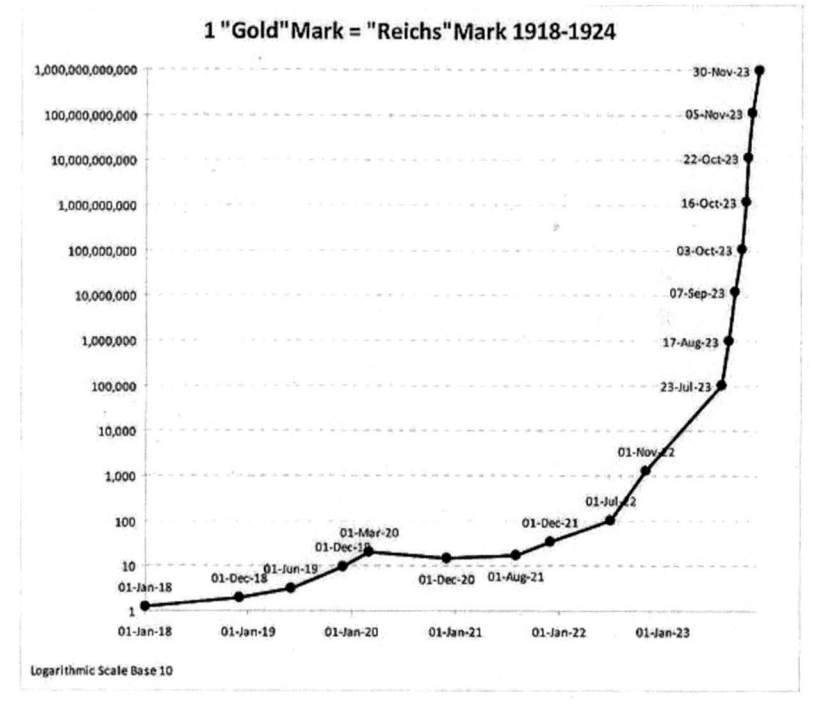

01-Jan-18	
01-Dec-18	
01-Jun-19	
01-Mar-20	
01-Dec-20	
01-Aug-21	
01-Dec-21	01-Jul-22
	01-Nov-22
23-Jul-23	
17-Aug-23	
07-Sep-23	
03-Oct-23	
16-Oct-23	
22-Oct-23	
05-Nov-23	
30-Nov-23	

Logarithmic Scale Base 10

Note: 1 "Gold"Mark value in grammes of fine gold (1913) = 0.35842g;
"Reichs"Mark = Currency not tied to the goldstandard in 1918 to 1924.

Source: *Law about the Revaluation of Mortgages and other Claims (Revaluation Act 1925), issued the 16th of July, 1925 (Aufwertungsgesetz, Reichsgesetzblatt, Teil I, 1925, p.133-135) and Author's calculations.*

The Weimar Republic was viewed as weak and fragile, spurring the development of many radical right wing parties. Many Germans connected the signing of the armistice to the Weimar Republic as Friedrich Ebert and others who had authorized the armistice played a role in the new republican government. Thus sprung the stab-in-the-back legend (*Dolchstosslegende*), which suggested that those who signed the armistice had surrendered German honor in a disgraceful peace. This theory, however, ignored that all German officers who served during World War I realized in November 1918 that the German army could no longer win on the battlefield, thus urging for a cease-fire.

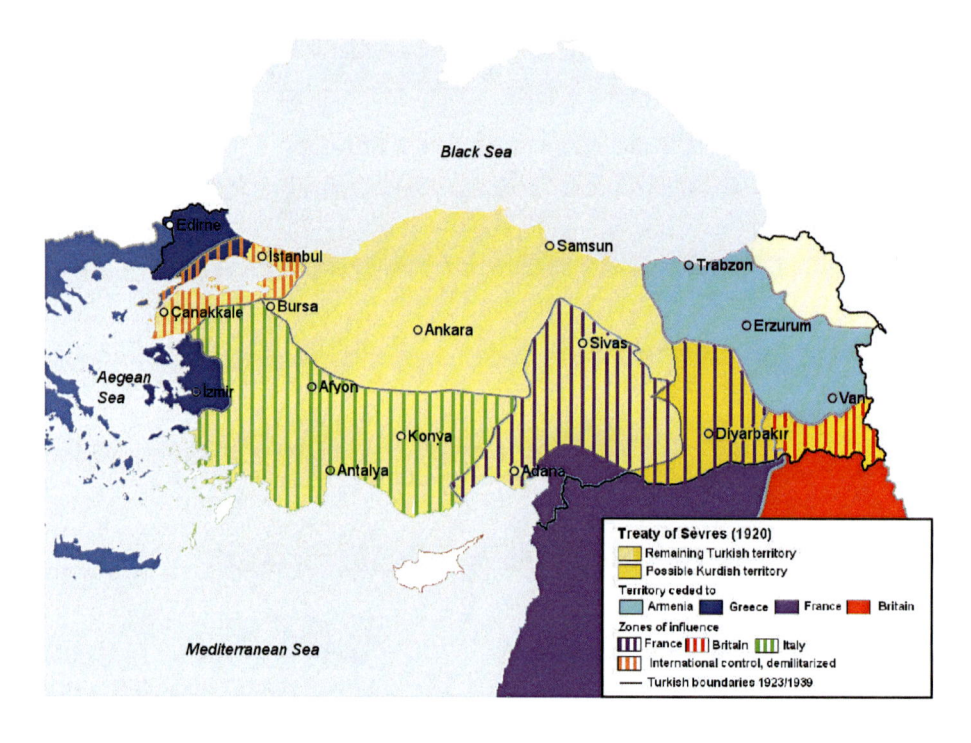

The Russian Revolution was also a direct consequence of World War I. Although some historians separate the connection between the Russian Revolution and World War I, instead pointing to the Russian Revolution of 1905, they are incorrect. Had Czar Nicolas II, who was seen as detached from the Russian people, not mishandled Russian involvement in World

War I, there most likely would not have been a Russian Revolution. By 1917, famine had swept across Russia and the people clamored for food and new leaders, turning first to a democratic-parliamentary government (March 1917) and later to a Communist system (November 1917).

The Ottoman Empire, which turned into Turkey, also experienced many changes. Mustafa Kemal Atatürk, a Turkish officer who helped repel the Allied invasion at the Dardanelles (much to Winston Churchill's chagrin), became a prominent figure in Turkey due to his military service and expertise. The Treaty of Sèvres, signed in 1920, had partitioned (and ultimately disintegrated) the Ottoman Empire. Atatürk began a nationalist revolution in Anatolia in May 1919 to protest the renunciation of non-Turkish territory and its cessation to Allied administration. The Turkish movement eschewed the significant loss of territory and eventually replaced the treaty of 1920 with the Treaty of Lausanne in 1923. Turkey gave up claims to the remainder of the Ottoman Empire and the Allies recognized Turkish sovereignty in the new borders.

In 1923, Turkey became a secular republic with Atatürk as its president. Under Atatürk, Turkey completely transformed. Previously, the Ottoman Empire had a culture quite different from that of Europe. Atatürk attempted to change that with a revolutionary program of social and political reform, embodied in his party's "six arrows": republicanism, nationalism, populism, statism, secularism, and revolution. Atatürk and his government abolished the caliphate and religious schools in 1924, abandoned the Islamic law code in 1926, replaced the Arabic script with the Latin alphabet in 1928, required the adoption of surnames or family in 1934, and gave women the right to vote in 1936. When Atatürk died in 1938, he was and continues to be extremely revered by the Turks. In Ankara, a mausoleum contains his sarcophagus and a museum dedicated to his memory. In fact, it is illegal to say anything against this founder of modern-day Turkey.

> **Did you know?**
> Atatürk was a name given to Mustafa Kemal by the Grand National Assembly of Turkey. It means "Father of the Turks." No politician or military leader in Turkey has ever surpassed the influence of Atatürk.

The United States became increasingly isolationist and pacifist, as demonstrated when the Senate's voted against joining the League of Nations. Just as George Washington had encouraged Americans to stay out of European affairs in his Farewell Address of 1796, the United States detached itself from European affairs. In fact, partially because Americans connected the war with Wilson and the Democratic Party, U.S. citizens elected three Republican presidents — who all promised to focus on domestic policy — in a row. The cultural and literary environment in the United States exploded in the 1920s with the Harlem Renaissance and the Roaring Twenties, best depicted by the flapper and F. Scott Fitzgerald's *The Great Gatsby*. American soldiers who had come back from the war had high hopes for the future, and their spending habits (along with the rest of the population) reflected their confidence.

> **Fun Fact**
>
> Ernest Hemingway was almost killed by a mortar attack during World War I and kept the piece of shrapnel the rest of his life in a small leather change purse.[150] Today, the shrapnel is on display in the John F. Kennedy Presidential Library. The war was always on Hemingway's heart, and many of his stories discuss how to respond to the "afterward."

While each country that fought experienced significant changes in response to the Great War, on a more individual level, families mourned and communities remembered. Although various countries had erected monuments after wars in the 19th centuries (for example, the many monuments of the American Civil War), the years after World War II saw a surge in the building of remembrances, except in the Soviet Union, which had left the war after the successful revolutions in 1917.[151] After the Treaty of Versailles was signed in 1919, the citizens of Kansas City "raised $2.5 million (roughly $35 million today) in just two weeks to build a monument."[152] Two years later in 1921, General Pershing and Harry Truman as well as other military commanders from France, Great Britain, Italy, and Belgium dedicated the site: "Ferdinand Foch, the French Marshal declared that he had never seen such patriotism."[153] Calvin Coolidge, who would later serve as President of the United States, also attended in 1921 and was invited in 1926 to officially recognize and dedicate the Liberty Memorial.

---

150. Putnam, 2006.
151. Audoin-Rouzeau and Becker, 2002.
152. Von Drehle, 2017.
153. Von Drehle, 2017.

> **Did you know?**
>
> Even years later, the citizens of Kansas City still maintain and appreciate their World War I monument: "In 1998, citizens voted to tax themselves for maintenance, and six years later they passed a bond issue to build an award-winning museum and research center beneath the memorial."[154]

Many monuments like those in northern France depicted the soldiers fighting honorably for their nation: "[T]he inhabitants chose Sacred Union monuments in bronze and stone, showing fighting *poilus* [the name for an infantry soldier in the French army, especially one that fought in World War I], triumphant roosters and home-front civilians struggling together for the victory of France."[155] In 1925, artist and war veteran Adolf Hitler even designed a monument to honor his fallen comrades, which was "a much larger arch of triumph than the one in Paris."[156]

Some areas, however, struggled with how to identify themselves. Alsace-Lorraine had rotated between French and German possession during the past 100 years, and their monuments reflected these difficulties: "In Alsace, soldiers are often represented naked on the monuments; for how can a German be distinguished from a Frenchman if he isn't wearing a uniform?"[157]

---

154. Von Drehle, 2017.
155. Audoin-Rouzeau and Becker, 2002.
156. Audoin-Rouzeau and Becker, 2002.
157. Audoin-Rouzeau and Becker, 2002.

Chapter 10: Conclusion (The Aftermath of the Armistice) 143

In addition to monuments, families and communities also grieved over loved ones by burying the dead. Until 1922, the bodies remained at cemeteries on the battlefield; after the summer of 1922, national law or decree gave Americans and French the right to request bodies to be sent home for burial. Other countries did not have the same rights. Almost 30 percent of the 700,000 identified bodies were requested and returned home.[158]

> **Did you know?**
>
> Veterans Day originally started as a commemoration of Armistice Day. On November 11, 1919, President Woodrow Wilson delivered a short address to remember the first anniversary of Armistice Day: "To us in America, the reflections of Armistice Day will be filled with solemn pride in the heroism of those who died in the country's service and with gratitude for the victory, both because of the thing from which it has freed us and because of the opportunity it has given America to show her sympathy with peace and justice in the councils of the nations..."[159] The United States Congress officially recognized Armistice Day with an act approved on May 13, 1938, making November 11 a national holiday. After World War II and the Korean War, Congress approved an amendment on June 1, 1954 to make November 11 a day to honor all veterans. For seven years from 1971 to 1978, Veterans Day was changed to a fixed Monday to ensure three-day weekends; in 1971, for example, Veterans Day was celebrated on October 25.[160] President Ford signed a law that took effect in 1978 that returned Veterans Day to its original day, November 11.[161]

Thus, in the end, studying World War I leaves us with several questions; some are counter-factual while others connect to World War II. First, was World War I "inevitable"? As a historian, the author prefers to avoid the word "inevitable" — it suggests a set view of history and does not allow for human action. World War I, or at the very least, a local conflict in the Balkans, was extremely likely. After all, there had already been two Balkan Wars in 1912 and 1913. Archduke Franz Ferdinand certainly helped hold everything together, but even his death did not necessitate a world war. The

---

158. Audoin-Rouzeau and Becker, 2002.
159. U.S. Department of Veterans Affairs.
160. U.S. Department of Veterans Affairs.
161. U.S. Department of Veterans Affairs.

Kaiser could have been more cautious in his willingness to assist Austria-Hungary, Austria-Hungary could have been less stringent in their terms, Germany could have stayed out of Belgium, and so on. But, as Dr. McMeekin points out in his various books and articles, it is hard to point fingers at the country that was responsible for the fomenting of World War I. Each country had a different aim and would risk war to achieve that aim. In this respect, World War II is much easier to understand because had there not been an Adolf Hitler, there would have been no Second World War. Thus, while the political climate in the 1910s was ripe for some kind of war, it did not necessarily have to be a world war that caused so much destruction in Europe.

Another question that many have discussed is German's ability to win: was there ever a point in which Germany was able to win? Although the German forces were certainly a force with which to be reckoned, their allies were sub par. Austria-Hungary quickly weakened, and the Ottoman Empire, Romania, Bulgaria, and others were all minor players. In essence, by 1917, the Germans were fighting three strong enemies — the United Kingdom, Russia, and the United States — by themselves. When Russia left the war in early 1918, Germany might have succeeded had United States soldiers not started to arrive in mass. This author would argue that as long as the United States stayed out of World War I, the Germans likely could have won. But, when America entered in April 1917, it brought many fresh, new troops that had not been in the trenches for several years. Despite its military prowess, Germany could not compete with the morale that the Americans brought, especially given that World War I had turned into a trench war with very little strategy or tactics after the first couple months of 1914.

Many people know that there was First World War (after all, there has to be one since there is a Second World War), but they know little about it. The Great War is overshadowed by World War II, leaving one to question: why is World War I remembered less than World War II? The author would say that it is likely because World War I happened earlier. Many prominent individuals during World War I had died by the time the Second World War ended. For those younger individuals in the First World War, they frequently had a greater presence in the Second World War, thus obscuring the time they served in the previous war. Another reason, at least for Americans, is that the United States entered World War I late compared to the other combatants. As a result, America sent fewer young men into battle and suffered fewer casualties. Finally, World War I only affected America indirectly; with World War II, especially in the Pacific theater, America had a direct interest. The Japanese had viciously attacked Americans at Pearl Harbor on December 7, 1941, a day that, according to President Roosevelt, would forever live in infamy. Many American families lost loved ones in the Second World War, making the war much more personal to them than the First World War. In the case of the author, her great-grandfather was drafted into the First World War, but avoided it due to his occupation as a farmer. Her grandfather, on the other hand, also was a farmer, but could not evade the draft and served in the Philippines for two years. Finally, in terms of military strategy, World War I has little to discuss. After the Schlieffen Plan and early months of fighting in late summer/early fall 1914, the Great War saw very few battles of tactical interest as all the fighting took place in trenches.

Finally, a famous phrase of the Great War — "the war to end all wars" — leaves us with a concluding question: why was the First World War not the war to end all wars? Rather than terminating war, World War I ushered in a century filled with killing and destruction from the Holocaust to the Armenian Genocide to Khmer Rouge in Cambodia. As you know, H.G. Wells penned the original phrase, "the war to end war," in a book discussing how the Great War would bring about a season of peace. Like many throughout history, Wells depicted the perennial human desire to have peace in the world. Perhaps due to the extent of the conflict, Wells believed that it might be more successful in issuing peace. And many shared his view. For many countries, the 1920s were a time of great economic development, social change, confidence, and peace. Or at least, so it seemed. With the stock market crash in 1929, the economic turmoil that ensued and the growth of totalitarian regimes in some countries, the high hopes for the end of the Great War were just wistful. In the end, World War I can teach us an important lesson: we should not trust that human beings are in a continual state of progress in which we will eventually reach a time on Earth when there is no war. War has always been with us and will always be with us. Instead, we should seek to understand the wars that have happened and their *casus belli* the best we can, which hopefully this book has done!

As Captain Griffith of the Welsh Fusiliers noted in his old age, the Great War had become impersonal, like the Trojan War of the ancient Greeks.[162] And it's true. World War I has become a forgotten war, much like the Korean War, both overshadowed by bigger conflicts that came later. Some of you may even have a grandparent or great-grandparent who fought in World War II. But World War I happened over 100 years ago, and it feels distant. The last American veteran of World War I, Frank Buckles, died in 2011 at 110 years old — everyone who remembers the Great War is now gone.

With any luck, this book has given you a taste of what the war was like, how the armistice was signed, the celebrations (or lack thereof) that ensued, and has encouraged you to learn more about the aspects of the Great

---

162. Persico, 2004.

War that interest you, thus combating the tendency for World War I to become detached .While, as Gil Petrina noted, the Trojan War has more tactical interest, understanding World War I is essential to having a good grasp of the twentieth century. World War II, the success of Communism in Russia, and the structure of Europe are all directly related to World War I. Now that you recognize the significance of the World War I armistice, you are way ahead of the game!

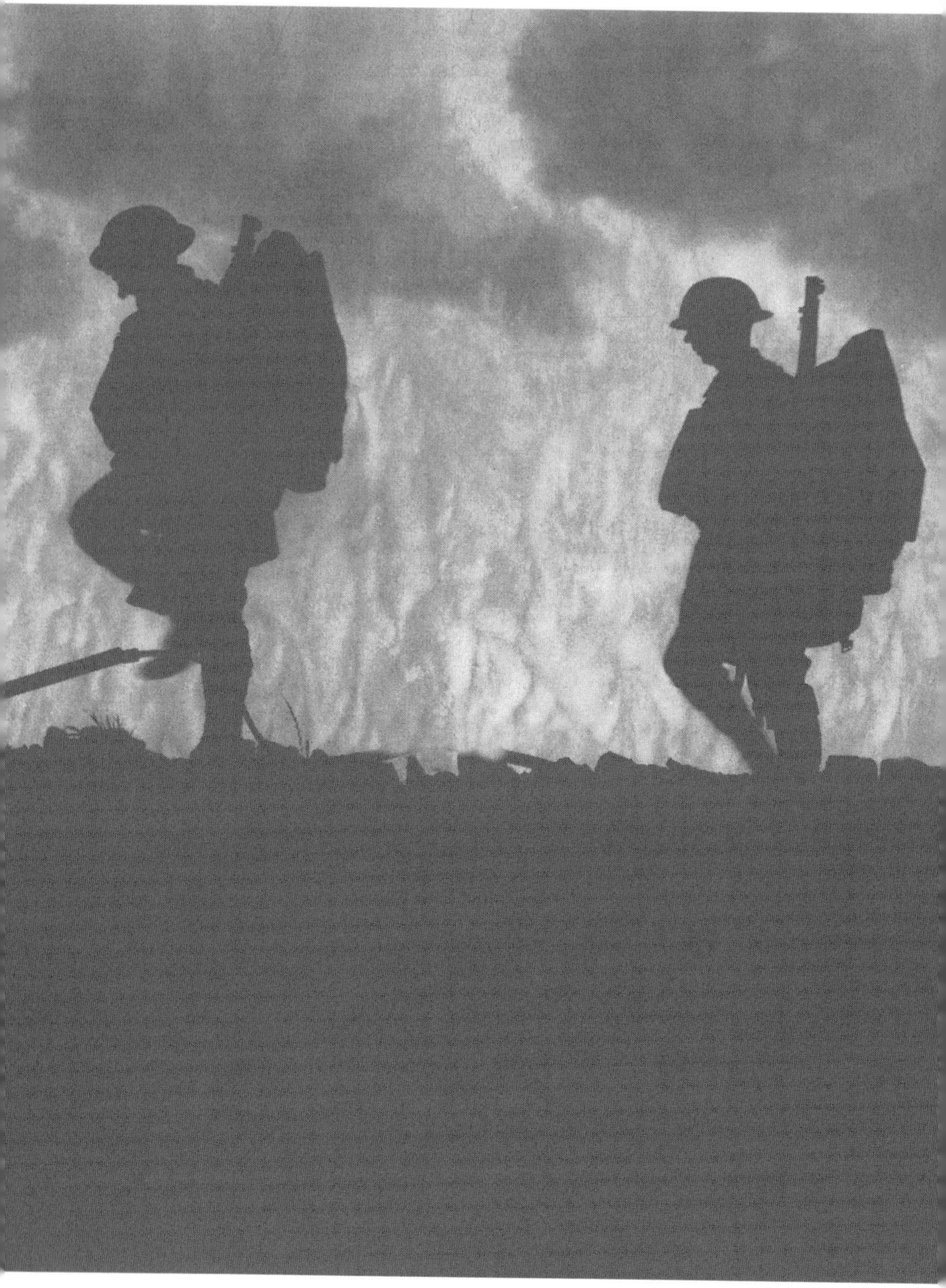

Author's Note/Acknowledgements

I have always enjoyed studying World War II, especially the Pacific Theater, because my grandfather fought in the Philippines and I remember his stories. World War I is definitely much less discussed than World War II, so I appreciated the opportunity to learn much more about the Great War. I realized in my study of World War I how much it was connected to the Franco-Prussian War of 1870-1871 and to World War II. I would argue that one cannot completely comprehend the modern world and the twentieth century without understanding the First World War. I was amazed at how many connections I noticed to World War I in my personal reading. From learning more about Churchill's sometimes overlooked role in World War I to a small comment about the Treaty of Versailles in national bestseller *Unbroken*, I had a better appreciation for what I read because I knew more about World War I.

I am extremely grateful to my friends and family for their support in my first foray into writing a book. I would like to especially thank several people for their assistance. Atlantic Publishing Company has been an ideal company with which to work. They were clear with directions, returned communications quickly, and were always able to answer any questions I had. My students, especially the class of 2017, gave me suggestions of what information to include in the book after we discussed World War I; it was quite helpful to know what a high school student would like to see in a book about the Great War. Audrey Southgate and Megan Korpics, who speak French and German respectively, assisted me with translations. I could always count on Christian Urch, one of my former students who is currently a history major at a local college, to help me verify any facts about the war, especially pertaining to weapons and military tactics. Gil and Carolyn Petrina regularly encouraged me in my work and frequently offered unique insights that I included in the book. Finally, I would like to thank my parents, Gary and LaRue Basinger, and my sister and brother-in-law, Rebekah and Daniel Slonim, for their continued support and encouragement. Rebekah, in particular, is the main reason I wrote this book. She told me that I could write a book, so I did.

I would highly encourage you to read more about World War I. Use this book as a starting point, a launch pad to further your studies of the war. I have included an extensive bibliography of sources that I used. If you notice that something you found intriguing has a footnote, see what book it came from and get that book from the library! I found several sources, in particular, extremely helpful. Joseph Persico's *Eleventh Month, Eleventh Day, Eleventh Hour* was my point of departure for this book. Mr. Persico included many interesting accounts and stories that made Armistice Day come alive for me. If you are interested in learning more about Winston Churchill and his role in English politics beyond World War I, Paul Johnson's *Churchill* was excellent. It is a short read, but extremely insightful. Sean McMeekin's *July 1914* brilliantly lays out the beginnings of the war. Dr. McMeekin has also written several articles and other books about World War I, which I would highly recommend. Finally, if you are interested in the wine regions in France and the impact World War I had on Champagne, *Champagne* by Don and Petie Kladstrup is one of the best works of history I have read. I would also recommend *Wine and War* if you wish to learn more about the German occupation of France during World War II. From Mr. and Mrs. Kladstrup I learned various, sundry details like unique ways the Allies in World War II learned of Nazi troop locations. The wine makers in France often received orders from the Third Reich for the Nazi troops and occasionally there would be specific instructions, such as, "package the wine for a hot climate." The wine makers knew that the Germans were most likely going to take over Italy's role in North Africa because all the other German fronts were in Europe, a much colder area.

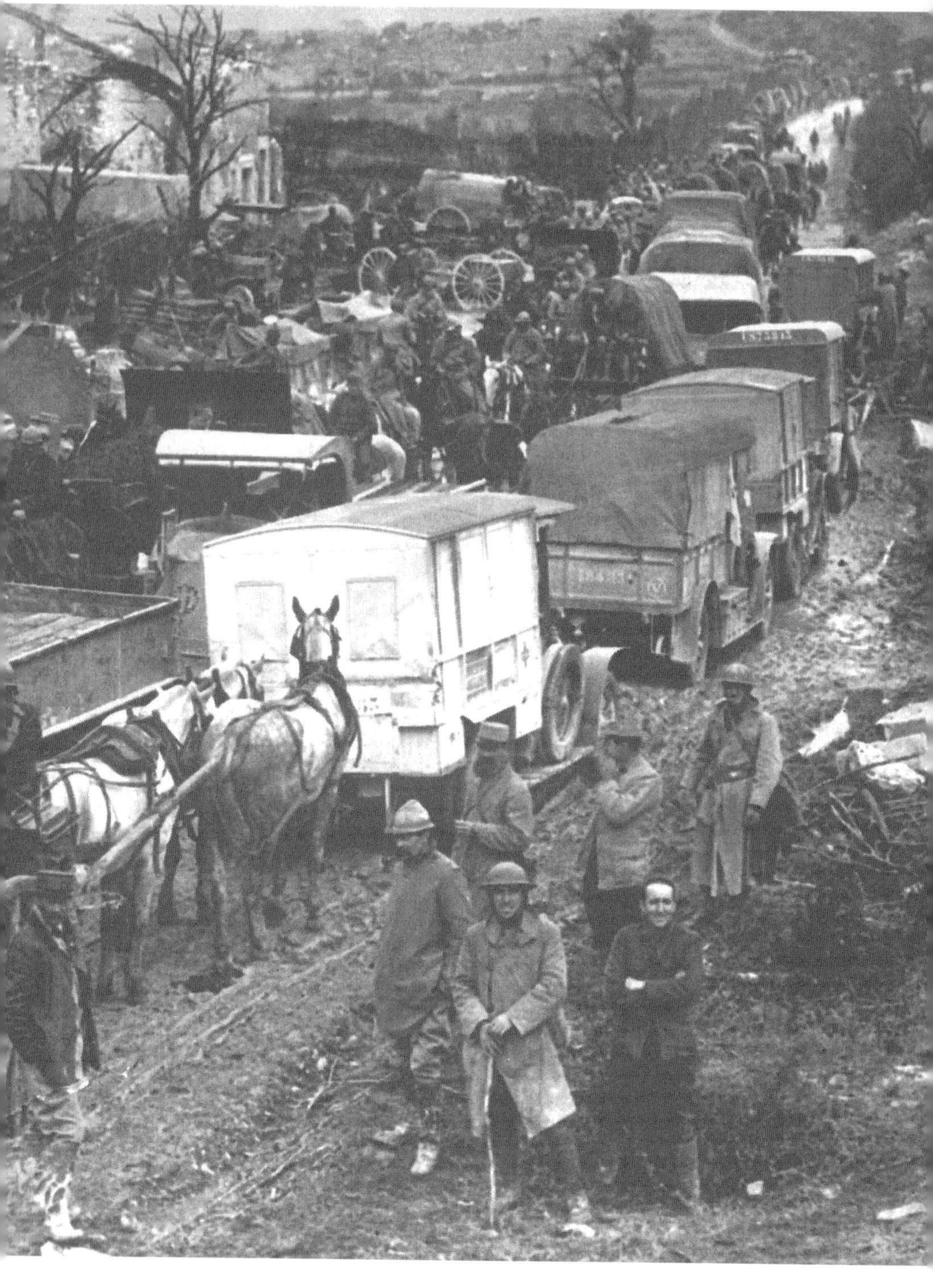

Historical Timeline

28 June 1914	Assassination of Archduke Ferdinand
6-10 September 1914	First Battle of the Marne
25 April 1915	Battle of Gallipoli
21 February - 18 December 1916	Battle of Verdun
1 July - 19 November 1916	Somme Offensive
31 July 1917 - 10 November 1917	Battle of Passchendaele (Third Battle of Ypres)
6 April 1917	United States Enters the War
18 July 1918	Second Battle of the Marne
11 November 1918	Armistice between Allies and Germany signed at 5:12 a.m.
18 January 1919 - 16 January 1920	Paris Peace Conference
28 June 1919	Peace of Versailles

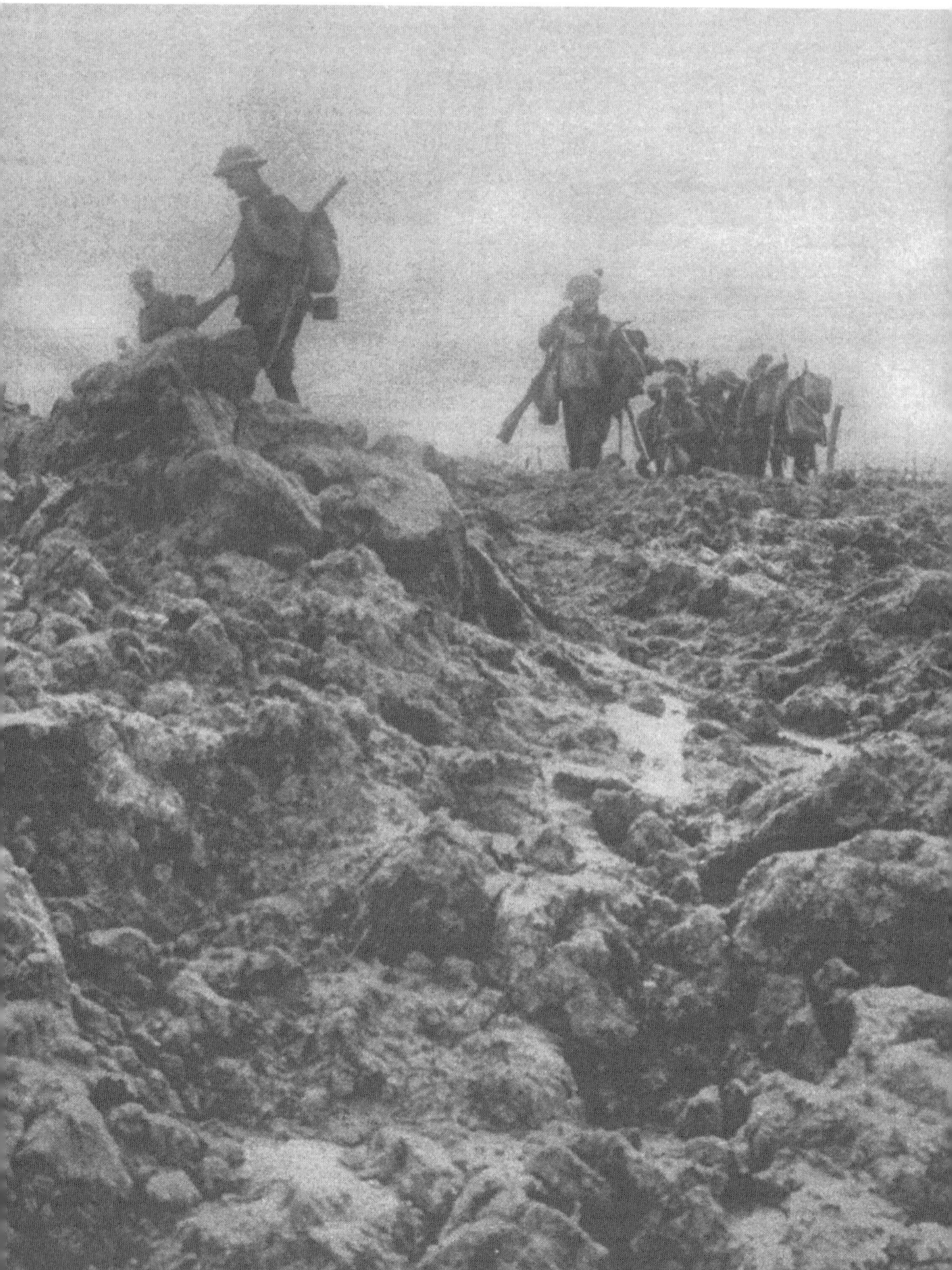

Glossary

Armistice: An armistice is a formal agreement made by warring parties to stop fighting for a certain time, or in other words, a truce, ceasefire, or suspension of hostilities. It is not necessarily the end of a war as it is a temporary peace.

Allied Powers: Originally consisting of the Triple Entente, the Allied Powers by the end of World War I would include Japan, the Yugoslav states, Italy (originally part of the Triple Alliance), Portugal, Romania, the United States, Central American states, Brazil, Greece, Siam, China, Liberia, and Armenia.

ANZAC: The Australian and New Zealand Army Corps (ANZAC), a part of the Mediterranean Expeditionary Force in World War I, was formed in Egypt in December 1914 and operated during the Battle of Gallipoli.

Boche: Used especially in military contexts during World War I (and World War II), Boche is an offensive term used to refer to a German, especially a German solider. Originally French slang, it is a variant of *Alboche*, meaning al (lemand) German (ca) boche blockhead.

Casualty: A casualty is a person killed or injured in a war or accident. Casualty is *not* synonymous with death.

Central Powers: The name "Central Powers" comes from the fact that all the member states of this alliance were located in between the Russian Empire in the east and France and the United Kingdom in the west. At the beginning of World War I, the Central Powers consisted of the German Empire and the Austro-Hungarian Empire. The Ottoman Empire and Bulgaria joined in 1914 and 1915 respectively.

Dardanelles: The Dardanelles, known in the ancient world as the Hellespont, is a narrow strait in modern day northwestern Turkey (or the Ottoman Empire during World War I) that forms part of the continental boundary between Europe and Asia.

Doughboy: An informal term used to refer to a member of the United States Army, especially members of the American Expeditionary Forces in World War I. The doughboys became youthful, iconic symbols for America.

Eastern Front: In contrast to the Western Front, the Eastern Front in World War I saw less action. It was the theater of operations that, at its greatest extent, included Russian and Romania on one side and Austria-Hungary, Bulgaria, the Ottoman Empire, and Germany on the other. The theater of war stretched from the Baltic Sea in the north and the Black Sea in the south and included most of Eastern Europe and some of Central Europe.

Flanders: A Dutch-speaking area that constitutes the northern half of Belgium, Flanders saw much of the fighting in the Western Front, centered on the town of Ypres. Canadian Lieutenant-Colonel John McCrae, inspired by his service during the Second Battle of Ypres, would popularize the region with his poem, "Flanders Field." Today Flanders Field is home to thousands of poppies. Additionally, on Armistice Day (November 11), most Britons wear a red poppy to symbolize the flowers blowing on the fields of Flanders.

Fontainebleau Memorandum: Written by British Prime Minister David Lloyd George and his advisers during the Paris Peace Conference on March 25, 1919, the Fontainebleau Memorandum was a document in which Lloyd George argued for more lenient post-war terms for Germany, stating that vindictiveness would only lead to the rise of Bolshevik propaganda in Germany. Additionally, harsh terms could also hurt the British people, as Germany had been Britain's second highest trading partner before the war. If the German economy were crippled, the British economy could suffer as well.

Hun: Used especially in military contexts during World War I (and World War II), Hun is a derogatory term that refers to a German or the Germans collectively (the Hun).

July crisis: A term used by historians to refer to the escalating political and military tensions in the summer of 1914, the July crisis began with the assassination of Archduke Franz Ferdinand on June 28, 1914 and ended on August 1, 1914 when Austria-Hungary declared war on Serbia (July 28, 1914), Russia and Germany declared war on each other, and France had ordered a general mobilization, now known as the day when the First World War erupted.

League of Nations: Inspired by President Woodrow Wilson's Fourteen Points, the League of Nations was founded in 1920 as a result of the Paris Peace Conference that ended World War I. Like its successor the United Nations, the League was the first international organization that maintained the primary goal of maintaining world peace. It existed from 1920 to 1946 although its power waned in the 1930s.

Ottoman Empire: Founded in the late 13th century and dismembered after the Ottoman defeat in the First World War, the Ottoman Empire was a vast amount of land in Europe, Asia, and Africa controlled by the Ottoman Turks.

Passchendaele: A village northeast of the Belgian town of Ypres, Passchendaele is the name often used to denote the Third Battle of Ypres from July to November 1917.

Poilu: An informal term for a French World War I infantry soldier, poilu literally means "hairy one." Today it is still used as a term of endearment for the French infantry of World War I.

Race to the Sea: The Race to the Sea took place from September 17 to October 19, 1914. The term depicts attempts by both the French and British and the German armies to surround the northern flank of the opposing army, rather than attempting to advance north toward the sea. While the outflanking attempts had resulted in a number of battles, neither side was able to gain a decisive victory, leading to the infamous trench warfare of World War I.

Rhineland: An industrial region in western Germany around the Rhine River, the Rhineland bordered France. Due to French concerns about Germany's ability to invade France through the Rhineland, Articles 42-44 of the Treaty of Versailles forbade Germany from stationing any military there.

Schlieffen Plan: The Schlieffen Plan was a battle plan first proposed by Alfred, Graf von Schlieffen, chief of the German general staff, at the request of the Kaiser. It would allow Germany to wage a successful two-front war against both France and Russia by eliminating one opponent quickly while keeping the other in check. Inspired by the Battle of Cannae in the Second Punic War, Schlieffen believed that a massive flank attack by modern forces could defeat a much larger force as Hannibal did with the

Romans. Schlieffen's successor, Helmuth von Moltke, made significant changes to the plan, including reducing the attacking force, which many suggest hindered Germany's ability to gain a quick victory.

Shell shock: A phrase coined in World War I to describe psychological disturbance caused by prolonged exposure to active warfare, shell shock especially referred to those under constant bombardment. In World War II, the name was changed to "battle fatigue."

Triple Alliance: Also known as the Triplice, the Triple Alliance was a secret agreement between Germany, Austria-Hungary, and Italy, formed in 1882. Italy however did not enter World War I on the side of the Central Powers, originally declaring neutrality and later entering the war on the Allied side.

Triple Entente: The Triple Entente was an agreement that linked the Russian Empire, the French Third Republic, and the United Kingdom after the signing of the Anglo-Russian Alliance in 1907. It was formed to counterbalance the threat posed by the Triple Alliance of Germany, Austria, and Italy of 1882.

Treaty of London: This treaty, signed by the Great Powers (including Great Britain) in 1839, promised to respect the independence and neutrality of Belgium. When Germany invaded Belgium on August 4, 1914 in violation of the treaty, Great Britain declared war on Germany that same day.

Weimar Republic: Named for the city in which the German government resided from 1919 to 1933, the Weimar Republic replaced the monarchical German state when Kaiser Wilhelm II abdicated on November 9, 1918.

Western Front: The Western Front was the main theater of war during World War I. After the German invasion of Belgium and the "Race to the Sea," both sides dug a line of trenches that stretched from the North Sea to the Swiss frontier with France. In other words, most of the fighting in World War I took place in Belgium and France. The line would stay roughly the same throughout the last four years of the war. One of the most prominent uses of this phrase is the translated English title of German veteran Erich Maria Remarque's novel about the extreme mental and physical stress German soldiers endured: *All Quiet on the Western Front*.

Wilsonianism: Named for President Woodrow Wilson, Wilsonianism is the idea that the world can be made "safe for democracy." Wilsonianism refers to Wilson's idealistic principles and his program to achieve a world without war.

Bibliography

Alston, Katharine. "How is the First World War Remembered?" *Imperial War Museums*, www.iwm.org.uk/learning/resources/how-is-the-first-world-war-remembered. Accessed 30 July 2017.

Audoin-Rouzeau, Stéphane, and Annette Becker. *14-18: Understanding the Great War*. Translated by Catherine Temerson. Hill and Wang, 2002, pp. 22-3; 168-9; 177; 183; 188; 201; 215; 228; 235-6.

Binding, Rudolf Georg. *A Fatalist at War*. Houghton Mifflin, 1929, p. 64.

"A Book for Every Man: The ALA Library War Service." *American Library Association Archives*, 2012, archives.library.illinois.edu/ala/ala-library-war-service/after-the-armistice. Accessed 21 July 2017.

Browder, Robert Paul. *Origins of Soviet American Diplomacy*. Princeton University Press, 2015, p. 208.

"The Cavalry Arm." *Times* [London, England] 5 June 1925, p. 8. *The Times Digital Archive*. Accessed 21 January 2017.

Chrystal, Paul. *Roman Military Disasters: Dark Days & Lost Legions*. Pen and Sword, 2015.

Clare, Sean. "WW1 mystery: Who killed Private John Parr?" *BBC News*, 4 August 2014, www.bbc.com/news/uk-28442670. Accessed 22 July 2017.

Clouting, Laura. "8 Celebrity Aces of the First World War." *Imperial War Museums*, www.iwm.org.uk/history/8-celebrity-air-aces-of-the-first-world-war. Accessed 21 July 2017.

Cosgrove, Ben. "Silence Visible: This is What the Sound of WWI's Ceasefire 'Looked' Like." *Time*, 18 November 2014, www.time.com/3881527/world-war-i-ceasefire-november-11-1918-graphic-2. Accessed 24 July 2017.

"D-Day and the Battle of Normandy: Your Questions Answered." *D-Day Museum*, 2015, http://www.ddaymuseum.co.uk/d-day/d-day-and-the-battle-of-normandy-your-questions-answered. Accessed 21 July 2017.

Dougall, Walter A. "20th-century international relations." *Encyclopedia Britannica*, 26 July 2017, www.britannica.com/topic/20th-century-international-relations-2085155/Peacemaking-1919-22. Accessed 29 July 2017.

Douglas, Allen. *War, Memory, and the Politics of Humor*. University of California Press, 2002, pp. 151-2.

"Entente, n." *OED Online*. Oxford University Press, December 2016. Accessed 12 January 2017.

Falls, Cyril. *The First World War*. Pen and Sword, 2014, p. 9.

Bibliography

"General George S. Patton's Military Career – Through WWI." *Armed Forces History Museum*, 26 March 2013, armedforcesmuseum.com/general-george-s-pattons-military-career-through-wwi/. Accessed 27 July 2017.

"Germany's hyperinflation phobia." *The Economist*, 15 November 2013. www.economist.com/blogs/freeexchange/2013/11/economic-history-1. Accessed 28 July 2017.

Gilbert, Martin. *Churchill: A Life*. Macmillan, 1992, pp. 483-4.

Gleit, Jon. "Armistice Day." Detroit Historical Society, 11 November 2015, blog.detroithistorical.org/2015/11/11/armistice-day/. Accessed 25 July 2017.

Gooch, G.P., and Harold Temperley, editors. *British Documents on the Origins of the War, 1898-1914*. Vol. XI. His Majesty's Stationery Office, 1926, p. 73.

Goya, Michel. *La chair et l'acier: L;armée française et l'invention de la guerre modern [Flesh and Steel: The French Army and the Invention of Modern Warfare]*. Tallandier, 2004.

"The Great War — Casualties and Deaths." *Public Broadcasting Service*, www.pbs.org/greatwar/resources/casdeath_pop.html. Accessed 15 June 2017.

Grey, Edward. "Great Britain and European Powers." *House of Commons*, 3 August 1914, pp. 1809-33, wwi.lib.byu.edu/images/6/67/Grey03081914.pdf. Accessed 21 January 2017.

Hayes-Fisher, John. "The last soldiers to die in World War I." *BBC News*, 29 October 2008. news.bbc.co.uk/1/hi/magazine/7696021.stm. Accessed 22 July 2017.

Hillenbrand, Laura. *Unbroken: A World War II Story of Survival, Resilience, and Redemption.* Random House, 2010, p. 31.

"History of Veteran's Day." *U.S. Department of Veterans Affairs,* www.va.gov/opa/vetsday/vetdayhistory.asp. Accessed 3 July 2017.

Jankowski, Paul. *Verdun: The Longest Battle in the War.* Oxford University Press, 2014, p. 4.

"Johnny | Johnnie, n." *OED Online.* Oxford University Press, December 2016. 12 January 2017.

Johnson, Paul. *Churchill.* Viking, 2009, pp. 39; 49; 55-6; 91-2.

———. *Modern Times Revised Edition: The World From the Twenties to the Nineties.* Harper Collins, 2010, pp. 26-27.

Kenney, Caitlin, and Zoe Chace. "The Economic Catastrophe That Germany Can't Forget." *NPR,* 14 September 2011. www.npr.org/sections/money/2011/09/14/140419140/the-economic-catastrophe-that-germany-cant-forget. Accessed 28 July 2017.

Kershaw, Robert. *24 Hours at the Somme.* Random House, 2016, pp. 173-4.

Kladstrup, Don, and Petie Kladstrup. *Champagne: How the World's Most Glamorous Wine Triumphed Over War and Hard Times.* Harper Perennial, 2006, pp. 13; 111; 218; 257-8.

Long, Public Papers, Container 2 (Diaries), Manuscript Division, Library of Congress, www.ctevans.net/Versailles/Archives/Long.html. Accessed 29 July 2017.

Lloyd, Nick. *Hundred Days: The Campaign that Ended World War I.* Basic Books, 2014.

McMeekin, Sean. *July 1914: Countdown to War.* Basic Books, 2014, pp. 6; 11; 13; 18

Miller, Paul. "The Sandwich that Sabotaged Civilisation." 10 January 2013. *University of Oxford* Podcasts, podcasts.ox.ac.uk/sandwich-sabotaged-civilisation. Accessed 15 January 2017.

Montgelas, Max, and Walther Schücking, editors. *Outbreak of the World War: German Documents Collected by Karl Kautsky*. Oxford University Press, 1924, pp. 78-79.

Mulvey, Paul. "Life in the Trenches: Soldiers on the Western Front, 1914-1918." Lecture, History 226, www.academia.edu/2129873/Life_in_the_Trenches_Soldiers_on_the_Western_Front_1914-1918_lecture_. Accessed 17 March 2017.

"The Murder of Archduke Franz Ferdinand at Sarajevo, 28 June 1914." *Eyewitness to History*, edited by John Carey, Avon, 1987, pp. 441-3.

"The Paris Peace Conference and the Treaty of Versailles." *Office of the Historian*, history.state.gov/milestones/1914-1920/paris-peace. Accessed 21 July 2017.

Patton, James. "Gas in the Great War." *University of Kansas Medical Center*, www.kumc.edu/wwi/essays-on-first-world-war-medicine/index-of-essays/medicine/gas-in-the-great-war.html. Accessed 20 January 2017.

Persico, Joseph E. *Eleventh Month, Eleventh Day, Eleventh Hour: Armistice Day, 1918: World War I and Its Violent Climax*. Random House, 2004.

Philadelphia War History Committee. *Philadelphia in the World War, 1914-1919*. Wynkoop Hallenbeck Crawford Company, 1922, p. 44.

Pitt, Barrie. *1918: The Last Act*. W.W. Norton, 1963, p. 8.

"Podcast 47: Armistice." *Imperial War Museums*, www.iwm.org.uk/history/podcasts/voices-of-the-first-world-war/podcast-47-armistice. Accessed 26 July 2017.

Putnam, Thomas. "Hemingway on War and Its Aftermath." *National Archives*, vol. 38, no. 1, Spring 2006. www.archives.gov/publications/prologue/2006/spring/hemingway.html. Accessed 21 August 2017.

"Presidential Job Approval Center." *Gallup*, www.gallup.com/interactives/185273/presidential-job-approval-center.aspx. Accessed 26 July 2017.

Richards, Grant. *A German Deserter's War Experiences*. Translated by J. Koettgen, B.W. Huebsch, 1917.

"City Went Wild, for a Great War Ended." Watertown *Daily Times*, 11 November 1952, www.watertownhistory.org/articles/ArmisticeDay1918.htm. Accessed 26 July 2017.

Roland, Helen. *Veteran's Day*. Miami-Dade College, 2011, faculty.mdc.edu/hroland/VeternsDay.htm. Accessed 20 January 2017.

Rudin, Harry. *Armistice 1918*. Yale University Press, 1944, pp. 426-432.

Rudmose-Brown, T. B. "Alsace-Lorraine: A Problem of Nationality." *Studies: An Irish Quarterly Review*, vol. 4, no. 15, 1915, pp. 367–383. www.jstor.org/stable/30092570.

Rudolph, Katie. "A Party in the Streets: Denver, Armistice Day, 1918." Denver Public Library, 12 November 2013, history.denverlibrary.org/news/party-streets-denver-armistice-day-1918. Accessed 26 July 2017.

Suddath, Claire. "Why Did World War I Just End?" *Time*, 4 October 2010, content.time.com/time/world/article/0,8599,2023140,00.html. Accessed 29 July 2017.

"Today in History – November 11: Veterans Day." Library of Congress, www.loc.gov/item/today-in-history/november-11. Accessed 25 July 2017.

"Unconditional Surrender Demand of Press of U.S.: No Armistice and No Agreements with Kaiser." *The Hartford Courant*, 14 October 1918, library.ccsu.edu/dighistFall16/files/original/4582c7cdcf7dcd1f46f b227291aba797.pdf Accessed 27 February 2017.

Von Drehle, David. "The world may little note, but Kansas City still remembers." *Time*, 17 April 2017, pp. 21-22.

Weber, Thomas. *Hitler's First War: Adolf Hitler, the Men of the List Regiment, and the First World War*. Oxford University Press, 2010, p. 222.

Wells, H.G. *The War That Will End War*. Duffield, 1914, p. 14.

Williams, Edie, and Alan R. Shaffer. "The Defense Innovation Initiative: The Importance of Capability Prototyping." *Joint Force Quarterly*, vol. 77, 2nd Quarter 2015, pp. 34-43. www.dtic.mil/doctrine/jfq/jfq-77.pdf.

Wilson, Woodrow. "Fourteen Points." Yale Law School Lillian Goldman Law Library, 8 January 1918, avalon.law.yale.edu/20th_century/wilson14. asp. Accessed 29 July 2017.

Zabecki, David T. *The German 1918 Offensives: A Case Study in the Operational Level of War*. Routledge, 2006.

Zuckerman, Larry. *The Rape of Belgium: The Untold Story of World War I*. NYU Press, 2004, p. 20.

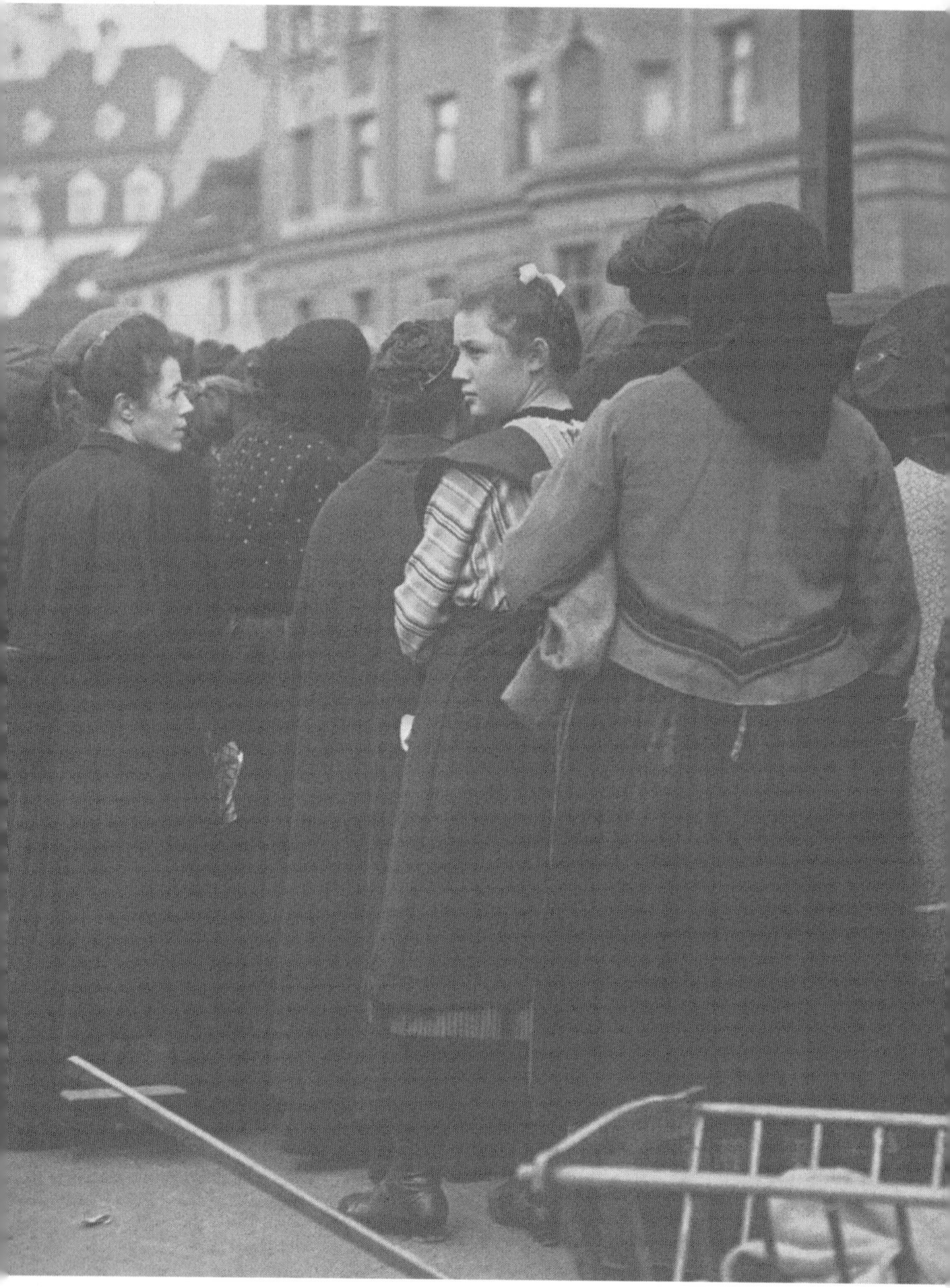

About the Author

Rachel Basinger teaches history and other humanities classes to ninth and twelfth graders at a small private school in Williamsburg, Virginia. She received a bachelor's degree in history from Hillsdale College in 2014. Many of the elective classes she took focused on modern history, and she wrote two undergraduate theses on Spanish anarchism and national identity in Spain and France. Her studies included examining Alsace-Lorraine during World War I and its promotion of French nationalism. A history buff, she loves to study nineteenth- and twentieth-century history, especially the World Wars and the Cold War.

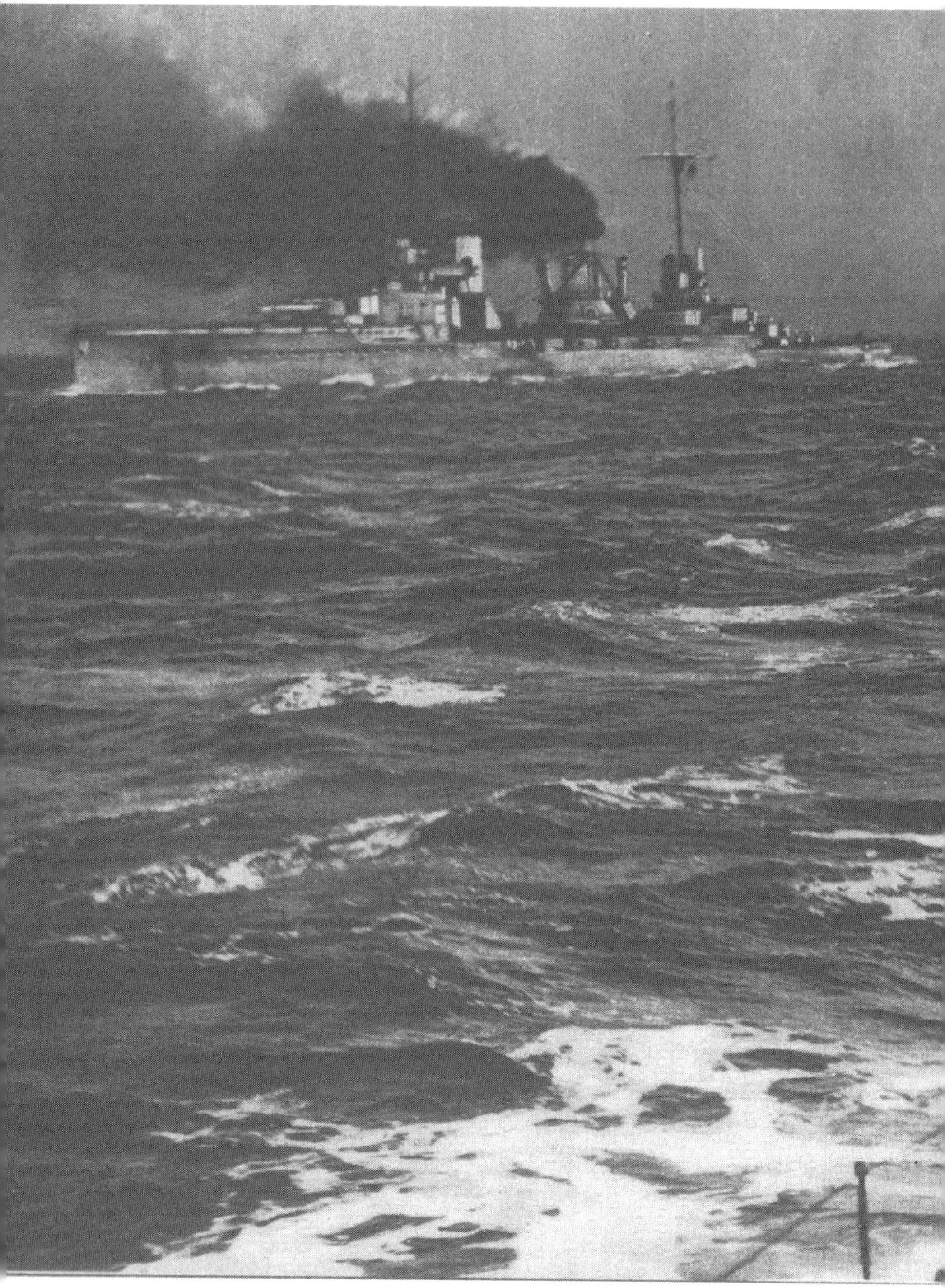

Index

A

Abdicate 63, 64
Aircraft 34, 35, 50, 91, 118
Allied Powers 5, 52, 107, 110, 131, 157
Alsace-Lorraine 28, 30, 56, 57, 67, 107, 113, 142, 168, 171
Africa 15, 83, 107, 153, 160
Archduke 21-24, 133, 144, 155, 159, 167
Asia 15, 107, 158, 160
Austria-Hungary 15-17, 19, 24-27, 51, 105, 107, 145, 158, 159, 161

B

Battlefield 11, 61, 83, 85, 95, 98, 138, 143
Battles 9, 15, 17, 39, 44, 51, 147, 160

C

Casualties 16, 74, 79, 81, 82, 146, 165
Campaign 36, 37, 42-44, 46, 50, 125, 166
Cease-fire 58-60, 69, 73, 80, 101, 138
Central Powers 15, 51, 105-107, 158, 161
Christmas 26, 33, 34, 135

Churchill, Winston 28, 36, 42, 44, 95, 125, 126, 135, 139, 152
Clemenceau, Georges 107, 108, 113

D

Disarmament 14, 111

F

Ferdinand, Franz 20, 21, 23, 144, 159, 167
Flanders 37, 38, 40, 158, 159
Fourteen Points 52, 55, 110, 111, 159, 169

G

Gas 15, 37, 38, 46, 48, 90, 130, 167
George Patton 122, 123

H

Hindenburg 17, 18, 45, 64-66, 83, 91, 92, 129
Hitler, Adolf 54, 71, 90, 117, 125, 128, 130, 142, 145, 169

K

Kaiser 9, 17, 18, 24, 25, 39, 46, 53, 57-59, 63-65, 90, 92, 99, 114, 128, 145, 160, 161, 168
Kaiserschlacht 9, 46

L

League of Nations 52, 53, 106, 108-111, 113, 116, 117, 140, 159
Ludendorff 9, 17, 18, 45, 46, 48, 52, 64, 71, 129

M

Mourning 10, 11, 92

N

No-Man's-Land 34, 42, 85

O

Ottoman Empire 15, 36, 107, 139, 145, 158, 160

P

Patton, George 122, 123
Paris Peace Conference 5, 15, 105, 106, 109, 115, 117, 155, 159, 167

R

Reparations 108-110, 113-116, 135
Rhineland 108, 113, 160
Russian Revolution 44, 46, 138, 139

S

Self-Determination 109
Serbia 15, 19, 21, 24-27, 107, 159

T

Treaty of Versailles 15, 70, 110, 111, 113, 116-118, 128, 130, 131, 133, 141, 151, 160, 167
Technology 15, 38
Trench Warfare 15, 31, 36, 160
Trenches 10, 31, 32, 34, 37, 42, 46, 103, 145, 147, 161, 167
Truman, Harry 88, 121, 141

V

Victory 25, 33, 39, 42, 48, 49, 51, 71, 95, 97, 99, 103, 108, 133, 135, 142, 144, 160, 161

W

Weimar Republic 65, 66, 91, 128, 138, 161
Western Front 9, 17, 31, 34-38, 44, 46, 77, 81, 82, 97, 98, 158, 161, 162, 167
Wilson, Woodrow 14, 18, 52, 101, 106, 107, 109, 144, 159, 162